Cambridge Direct Mathematics

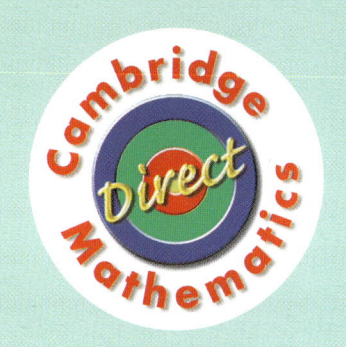

Measures, Shape, Space and Handling Data

6

CAMBRIDGE UNIVERSITY PRESS

PUBLISHED BY THE PRESS SYNDICATE OF THE UNIVERSITY OF CAMBRIDGE
The Pitt Building, Trumpington Street, Cambridge, United Kingdom

CAMBRIDGE UNIVERSITY PRESS
The Edinburgh Building, Cambridge CB2 2RU, UK
40 West 20th Street, New York, NY 10011-4211, USA
10 Stamford Road, Oakleigh, VIC 3166, Australia
Ruiz de Alarcón 13, 28014 Madrid, Spain
Dock House, The Waterfront, Cape Town 8001, South Africa

http://www.cambridge.org

© Cambridge University Press 2001

First published 2001

Printed in the United Kingdom at the University Press, Cambridge

Typefaces Frutiger, Helvetica, Minion, Swift *System* QuarkXPress®4.03

A catalogue record for this book is available from the British Library

ISBN 0 521 78496 4 paperback

Text illustration Gary Rees

General editors for *Cambridge Mathematics Direct*
Sandy Cowling, Jane Crowden, Andrew King, Jeanette Mumford

Writing team for *Measures, Shape, Space and Handling Data 6*
Anne Barber, Salliann Coleman, Roger Gee, Claire Grigson, Gill Hatch, Sue Hood, Bob La Roche, Clare Lauritzen, Kerry Lundy, Jeanette Mumford, Mary Nathan, Madeline Swarbrick, Allison Toogood, Elizabeth Toohig, Jane Webster, Joanne Woodward

The writers and publishers would like to thank the many schools and individuals who trialled lessons for Cambridge Mathematics Direct.

NOTICE TO TEACHERS
It is illegal to reproduce any part of this work in material form
(including photocopying and electronic storage) except under
the following circumstances:
(i) where you are abiding by a licence granted to your school or institution by
the Copyright Licensing Agency;
(ii) where no such licence exists, or where you wish to exceed the terms of a
licence, and you have gained the written permission of Cambridge
University Press;
(iii) where you are allowed to reproduce without permission under the
provisions of Chapter 3 of the Copyright, Designs and Patents Act 1988.

Abbreviations and symbols

IP Interactive picture

CM Copymaster

A is practice work

B develops ideas

C is extension work

★ if needed, helps with work in A

A red margin indicates that activities are teacher-led.
A green margin indicates that activities are independent.

Contents

Measures (M)

M1 Length
M1.1 Rounding distances and lengths — 5
M1.2 Converting kilometres to smaller units — 6
M1.3 Metric and imperial units — 7
M1.4 Reading scales and solving problems — 9

M2 Mass
M2.1 Relationships and rounding — 11
M2.2 Converting between kilograms and grams — 14
M2.3 Metric and imperial units — 17
M2.4 Reading scales and solving problems — 20

M3 Capacity
M3.1 Litres and millilitres — 24
M3.2 Rounding capacity measurements — 26
M3.3 Metric and imperial capacities — 28
M3.4 Capacity problems — 30

M4 Area and perimeter
M4.1 Perimeters of compound shapes — 32
M4.2 Areas of compound shapes — 33
M4.3 Surface areas — 35
M4.4 Areas of isosceles triangles — 37
M4.5 Area of right-angled triangles — 39

M5 Time
M5.1 World time zones — 41
M5.2 Time zones and date changes — 43
M5.3 Solving time problems — 45

Shape and space (SS)

SS1 Properties of 2-D shapes
SS1.1 Parallelograms and rhombuses — 47
SS1.2 Trapeziums and kites — 49
SS1.3 Diagonals — 51
SS1.4 Circles — 53
SS1.5 Tangrams — 54
SS1.6 Reasoning about shapes — 55

SS2 Properties of 3-D shapes
SS2.1 Properties of 3-D shapes — 57
SS2.2 Nets for closed cubes — 58
SS2.3 Visualising 3-D shapes — 59

SS3	**Reflective symmetry**	
SS3.1	Reflections in 1 mirror line	61
SS3.2	Reflections in 2 mirror lines	62
SS3.3	Reasoning about symmetry	63
SS4	**Translation**	
SS4.1	Translations and 3-D shapes	64
SS4.2	Translating patterns	66
SS4.3	Translations in 4 quadrants	68
SS4.4	Translating and tessellating	70
SS5	**Position and direction**	
SS5.1	Intersecting lines	71
SS5.2	Beyond the first quadrant	73
SS5.3	Plotting co-ordinates in all 4 quadrants	74
SS5.4	Patterns in co-ordinates	76
SS6	**Angle and rotation**	
SS6.1	Measuring angles	77
SS6.4	Reflex angles	78

Handling data (HD)

HD1	**Probability**	
HD1.2	Finding probabilities	80
HD1.3	Using a 0–1 scale for probabilities	83
HD1.4	Experimenting to find probabilities	85
HD2	**Organising and interpreting data 1**	
HD2.2	Mean, median, mode and range 1	87
HD2.3	Pie charts 1	89
HD2.4	Line graphs 1	91
HD3	**Organising and interpreting data 2**	
HD3.1	Testing a hypothesis 2	92
HD3.2	Mean, median, mode and range 2	93
HD3.3	Pie charts 2	95
HD3.4	Line graphs 2	96
HD4	**Organising and interpreting data 3**	
HD4.2	Mean, median, mode and range 3	99
HD4.3	Interpreting and comparing data	101
HD4.4	Line graphs 3	103

M1.1 Rounding distances and lengths

> **Key idea** In certain situations an approximate measure, to the nearest whole unit or tenth of a unit is needed.

A1 Write the distance to each place to the nearest kilometre.

a Greenford 7.1 km b Newton 10.8 km c Avondale 22.5 km

A2 Spectators at a football match compare the distances they have travelled.
Round to the nearest kilometre.

a 126.78 km b 142.35 km c 78.49 km d 0.83 km e 28.29 km

A3 Jane measured the thickness of some library books.
Roughly how many centimetres are they to the nearest whole centimetre?

a 47 mm b 25 mm c 12 mm d 36 mm e 109 mm

A4 Do CM 1.

B1 Cyclists travelled these distances in training.
Approximately how far did they cycle to the nearest kilometre?

a 7628 m b 13 509 m c 9398 m d 14 901 m e 7489 m

B2 Anil measured some objects in his classroom.
About how many metres are they to the nearest tenth of a metre?

1 cm = 0.01 m

a 113 cm b 45 cm c 67 cm d 26 cm e 98 cm

C1 An experiment to grow plants produced the following results.
Round the heights of each plant to the nearest tenth of a metre.

a 280 mm b 576 mm c 231 mm d 84 mm e 347 mm

M1 Length

M1.2 Converting kilometres to smaller units

> **Key idea** | 1 m is one thousandth of 1 km.

A1 A chart gives the height above sea level of several towns.

Write these heights in metres.

- **a** 0.003 km
- **b** 0.007 km
- **c** 0.016 km
- **d** 0.080 km
- **e** 0.668 km
- **f** 0.900 km

A2 **You need 5 objects smaller than your hand to measure.**

Record your measurements in centimetres and then convert them to metres.

B1 Which of the two measurements is higher above sea level?

- **a** 3.59 km or 450 m
- **b** 2978 m or 4.66 km
- **c** 0.04 km or 20 m
- **d** 70 m or 0.01 km

B2

Map showing distances from Wellby:
- Barford 7.5 km
- Appleton 3 km
- Castleborough 6.9 km
- Deerthorpe 3.25 km
- Eastwell 9.04 km
- Fullbrook 8.35 km

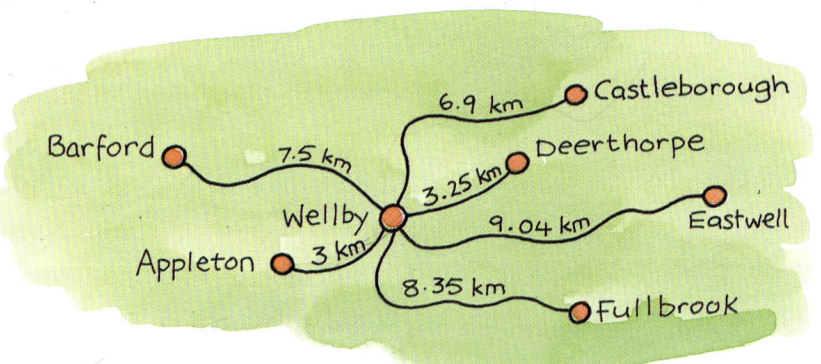

How far is it in metres from Wellby to:

- **a** Appleton?
- **b** Barford?
- **c** Castleborough?
- **d** Deerthorpe?
- **e** Eastwell?
- **f** Fullbrook?

Convert all lengths to metres.

B3 Arrange these lengths in order from smallest to largest.

0.041 m   0.003 km   0.1 cm   5.082 m   128 mm   491 cm

C1 **You need 5 objects less than 100 mm long and a ruler marked only in millimetres.**

Measure your objects in millimetres then convert to metres.

M1.3 Metric and imperial units

Key idea	A mile is about 1600 m. 8 km is about 5 miles.
	A metre is longer than a yard. A metre is about 3 feet 3 inches.

You need your graph and a partner.

British drivers travelling in Europe need to convert distances given in kilometres into miles. Use your graph to convert the distances in the following problems.

1 Convert these distances into kilometres.

    a 10 miles   **b** 25 miles   **c** 50 miles   **d** 75 miles

2 Use your graph to find which is further:

    a 5 miles or 6 km   **b** 28 km or 15 miles

    c 56 km or 36 miles   **d** 81 km or 49 miles

3 Complete these, choosing from the list below.

    a 12 inches =   **b** 2 feet =   **c** $\frac{1}{2}$ foot =

    d 1 yard =   **e** 1 metre =   **f** 2 metres =

    6 inches   3 feet   1 foot   24 inches $6\frac{1}{2}$ feet   3 feet 3 inches

4 **a** List 3 classroom objects that you would measure in inches and 3 objects that you would measure in feet.

    b What imperial unit would you use to measure the height of a door?

M1 Length

5 Put these distances in order, from shortest to longest:

10 miles   45 km   15 miles   20 km   25 miles   15 km

6
a John travelled 11 miles. How many kilometres did he go?

b Calais is 38 km away. How far is this in miles?

c It is 95 km to Paris. Morag has travelled 56 miles. How much further has she to go?

d Lenny drives 21 miles from his campsite to Beauville. Then he drives 18 miles to the beach and goes straight home to the campsite from there. If his total journey was about 75 km that day, what is the distance in kilometres from the campsite to the beach?

7 Choose from <, >, = to complete these questions.

a 6 feet ☐ 2 m   **b** 3 m ☐ 9 feet 9 inches

c 3 yards ☐ 11 feet   **d** 13 feet ☐ 4 metres

e 20 m ☐ 20 yards   **f** 1 foot ☐ 20 inches

Remember:
1 foot = 12 inches
1 yard = 3 feet

8 Make up 3 of your own number problems using imperial and metric units.

Key idea	A mile is about 1600 m. 8 km is about 5 miles.
	A metre is longer than a yard. A metre is about 3 feet 3 inches.

8   M1 Length

M1.4 Reading scales and solving problems

| Key idea | You need to choose the right scale to measure in metric or imperial units. |

1 Sarah travelled 34.24 km by car, 2.7 km by bus and 1000 m on foot. How many kilometres did she travel?

2 I cut 65 cm off 3.5 m of rope. How much is left?

3 A class measured rainfall using rain gauges they made themselves. Some scales were in inches, others in centimetres. Use the scale to answer these questions.

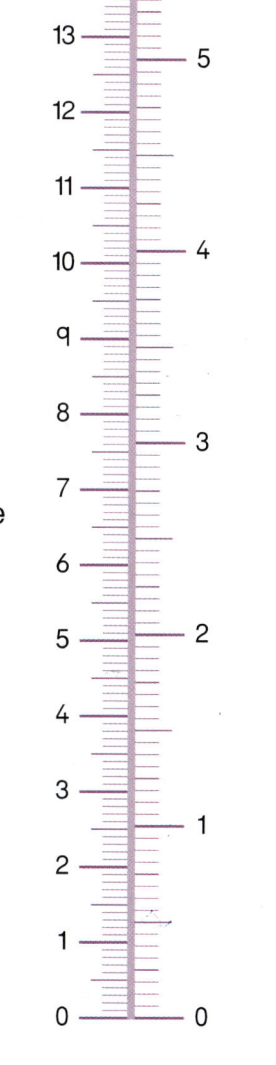

    a On Monday there was 1 inch of rain.

    How many centimetres is this?

    b On Tuesday there was $\frac{1}{2}$ inch of rain.

    How many centimetres is this?

    c On Wednesday and Thursday it didn't rain, but on Friday there were $1\frac{1}{4}$ inches of rain.

    How many centimetres is this?

    d What was the total rainfall for these 5 days in centimetres?

4 The next week it rained 1.7 cm on Monday. If it rained the same amount every day until Friday, how many inches of rain fell on these 5 days?

5 If the total rainfall for 10 days was 5 inches, what was the average rainfall each day? Give your answers in centimetres.

M1 Length

6 The third week Nadim measured 1.8 cm, 0.4 cm, 5.1 cm, 0.3 cm and 2.6 cm of rain.

a What was the total rainfall for the 5 days in centimetres?

b How much is this to the nearest $\frac{1}{4}$ inch?

c The school weather station recorded exactly $1\frac{1}{2}$ inches of rainfall.

Which child had the most accurate rain gauge?

Josh 3.5 cm   Kay 3.8 cm   Mansi 3.4 cm   Nadim 3.6 cm

7 In the fourth week, Monday had 1.2 cm of rain, Tuesday $\frac{3}{8}$ inch, Wednesday 2.4 cm, Thursday $\frac{7}{8}$ inch and Friday 2.5 cm.

a Which day did it rain the most?

b Which day did it rain the least?

c What was the total rainfall in centimetres?

d What was the total rainfall in inches?

8 The average rainfall for the fifth week was $\frac{3}{4}$ inch of rain over the 5 days.
Rainfall on Monday was 1.1 cm below average, on Tuesday 0.5 cm above average, on Wednesday 1.6 cm above average and on Thursday 1.0 cm below average.

a Give the total rainfall in centimetres for week 5.

b Work out the rainfall in inches each day that week including Friday.

9 A bow is made from 6 inches of ribbon.

How many bows can be made from 3 m of ribbon?

10 There are 2.54 cm to 1 inch. 1 yard is 36 inches.

About how many centimetres are there in 1 yard?

Key idea	You need to choose the right scale to measure in metric or imperial units.

M1 Length

M2.1 Relationships and rounding

> **Key idea** 1 tonne is 1000 kg.

A1 Look at these items. Write the mass that would be most appropriate for each one.

a) 30 g   3 kg   30 kg

b) 450 g   4.5 kg   45 kg

c) 250 tonnes   2.5 kg   25 kg

d) 36 kg   360 kg   3.6 tonnes

e) 2.7 g   27 g   270 g

f) 150 g   1.5 kg   15 kg

A2 A zoo orders food supplies for the animals. Copy and complete the following table.

Food	Mass	Mass in tonnes	Rounded to the nearest tenth of a tonne
fruit	2470 kg		
vegetables	2010 kg		
meat	1650 kg		
fish	1160 kg		
grains	2920 kg		
hay	1535 kg		

M2 Mass

B1 A fizzy drinks factory sells drinks in crates. It makes 7.186 tonnes of cola crates, 5.573 tonnes of lemonade crates, 3.918 tonnes of orangeade crates, 3.354 tonnes of cherryade crates and 2.019 tonnes of ginger beer crates.

a Convert each mass to kilograms to find the total mass in kilograms.

b Now round the mass of each type of drink to the nearest tonne.

c Use these rounded masses to find approximately how many tonnes of drinks crates were sold in total.

d Convert your answer to **c** to kilograms. Compare this with the total mass you found in **a**.

Each full drinks crate weighs 25 kg. A van can hold 24 crates. A lorry can hold 120 crates.

e How many tonnes of drink can 1 lorry deliver?

f How many tonnes of drink can 1 van deliver?

g How many lorries or vans would be needed to deliver each type of drink?

B2 Here is a list of things you might want to take on your trekking holiday.

a Copy and complete this table.

Item	Weight	Weight in kilograms	To nearest kilogram	To nearest tenth of a kilogram
Books	1239 g			
Sweets and snacks	1050 g			
Clothes	7354 g			
Walking boots	1371 g			
Sleeping bag	2128 g			
Rain gear	966 g			
Wash kit	835 g			

Your empty backpack weighs 1.5 kg.

b What is the total mass of your full backpack in grams?

c What is the mass of your full backpack rounded to the nearest kilogram?

d What is the mass of your full backpack rounded to the nearest tenth of a kilogram?

e Is there an excess baggage charge due?

C1 A plane holds 410 people. Every passenger has 20 kg of check-in luggage and 10 kg of hand luggage.

a How many tonnes of check-in luggage will be on the plane?

b How many tonnes of hand luggage will be on the plane?

C2 Every passenger is given a blanket weighing 190 g, a cushion weighing 176 g, a free drink weighing 181 g and a meal weighing 522 g.

What is the total mass to the nearest tenth of a kilogram of:

a blankets? **b** cushions? **c** drinks? **d** meals? **e** all 4 items?

C3 How many tonnes do all the luggage, blankets, cushions, drinks and meals weigh altogether, to the nearest tenth of a tonne?

Key idea 1 tonne is 1000 kg.

M2 Mass

M2.2 Converting between kilograms and grams

Key idea	1 g is one thousandth of 1 kg.

Here are the contents of a shopping basket.

- Breakfast Flakes — 375 g
- Beans — 450 g 
- Biscuits — 150 g 
- Potatoes — 3.5 kg  
- Sugar — 1.5 kg 
- Doughnut — 58 g
- Flour — 1.3 kg 
- Crisps — 27 g 
- Choc bar — 75 g 

★1 Charcoal weighs 5 kg. This is 5000 g. What is the mass in grams of the:

　a potatoes?　　b sugar?　　c flour?

★2 Coffee weighs 250 g. This is 0.250 kg. What is the mass in kilograms of the:

　a cereal?　　b beans?　　c biscuits?

★3 Herbs weigh 72 g. This is 0.072 kg. What is the mass in kilograms of the:

　a crisps?　　b chocolate bar?　　c doughnut?

★4 Find the total mass of the heaviest item and lightest item in grams.

★5 Find the total mass of all the shopping in kilograms.

★6 What is this total in grams?

A1 You need scales, objects to weigh and a partner.

Draw this table in your book.

Item	Estimated mass		Actual mass		Difference	
	kg	g	kg	g	kg	g
dictionary	1.5	1500	1.865	1865	0.115	115
pencil						
shoe						
scissors						
ruler						

Estimate and record the mass of each item in kilograms and grams. The first one has been done for you.

Now weigh each item and record its actual mass in kilograms and grams.

Calculate the difference between the estimated mass and the actual mass in kilograms and grams.

Now find 2 more items and repeat the process for them.

B1 Here is a table showing the mass of some coins.

Coin	£2	£1	50p	20p	10p	5p	2p	1p
Mass	12 g	9.5 g	8 g	5 g	6.5 g	3.25 g	7.13 g	3.56 g

What is the mass in kilograms of:

a £1 in 1p coins?

b £2 in 2p coins?

c £5 in 5p coins?

d £10 in 50p coins?

e £10 in £1 coins?

f £10 in £2 coins?

Calculate first then convert to kg.

M2 Mass

B2 Give the mass in kilograms of the coins in a purse containing:

  a a 50p and a 20p

  b a £1 and a 10p

  c three 5p coins, a 2p and two 1p coins

B3 A bag contains 50 coins all of the same value. If it has a mass of 0.325 kg, which type of coin is in the bag?

B4 A bag contains 20p coins. If the coins have a mass of 0.485 kg, how many coins are in the bag?

B5 You collect all your 20p and 50p coins in a money box. The empty box has a mass of 120 g. It now weighs 0.64 kg.

  a If the box contains only 20p coins, how many are in the money box?

  b If the box contains only 50p coins, how many are in the money box?

  c If there are equal numbers of 20p and 50p coins in the box, how much are the coins worth altogether?

Key idea 1 g is one thousandth of 1 kg.

M2.3 Metric and imperial units

Key idea	30 g is about an ounce (oz). 1 kg is about 2.2 pounds (lb).

★1 You need scales and objects to weigh.

Weigh several objects to find objects with a mass of about 1 oz, 2 oz, 3 oz, 4 oz, 8 oz and 1 lb.

Copy and complete this chart. Weigh your objects to find the masses in grams.

Approximate mass in ounces	Objects	Approximate mass in grams
1 oz		
2 oz		
3 oz		
4 oz		
8 oz		
1 lb		

★2 Which is heavier:

a. 2 oz or 50 g? b. 3 oz or 100 g?

★3 How many pounds are the same as 1 kg?

A1 How many ounces are there in each of these masses?

a. $\frac{1}{2}$ lb b. $\frac{3}{4}$ lb c. $1\frac{1}{4}$ lb d. $2\frac{1}{2}$ lb

Remember:
1 lb = 16 ounces

A2 How many pounds (lb) and ounces (oz) are there in each of these?

a. 4 oz b. 32 oz c. 24 oz d. 48 oz

A3 Do CM 8.

A4 Use your scale to find out roughly how many grams in:

a. 2 oz b. 7 oz c. 9 oz d. $\frac{3}{4}$ lb e. 10 oz

M2 Mass

B1 Here is a list of ingredients needed to make toffee bars.

Copy it into your book, converting the imperial masses into metric masses.

Toffee bars
- 4 oz margarine
- 2 oz caster sugar
- 3 oz brown sugar
- 8 oz self-raising flour
- 6 oz rolled oats
- 2 oz plain chocolate
- 1 oz chopped nuts
- 1 egg

Some families from a school have been making jam for the school fair. Unfortunately, not all the jars are the same size and some have been labelled in metric units and others in imperial units. Use the line graph below to help you answer the following questions:

Converting pounds and kilograms.

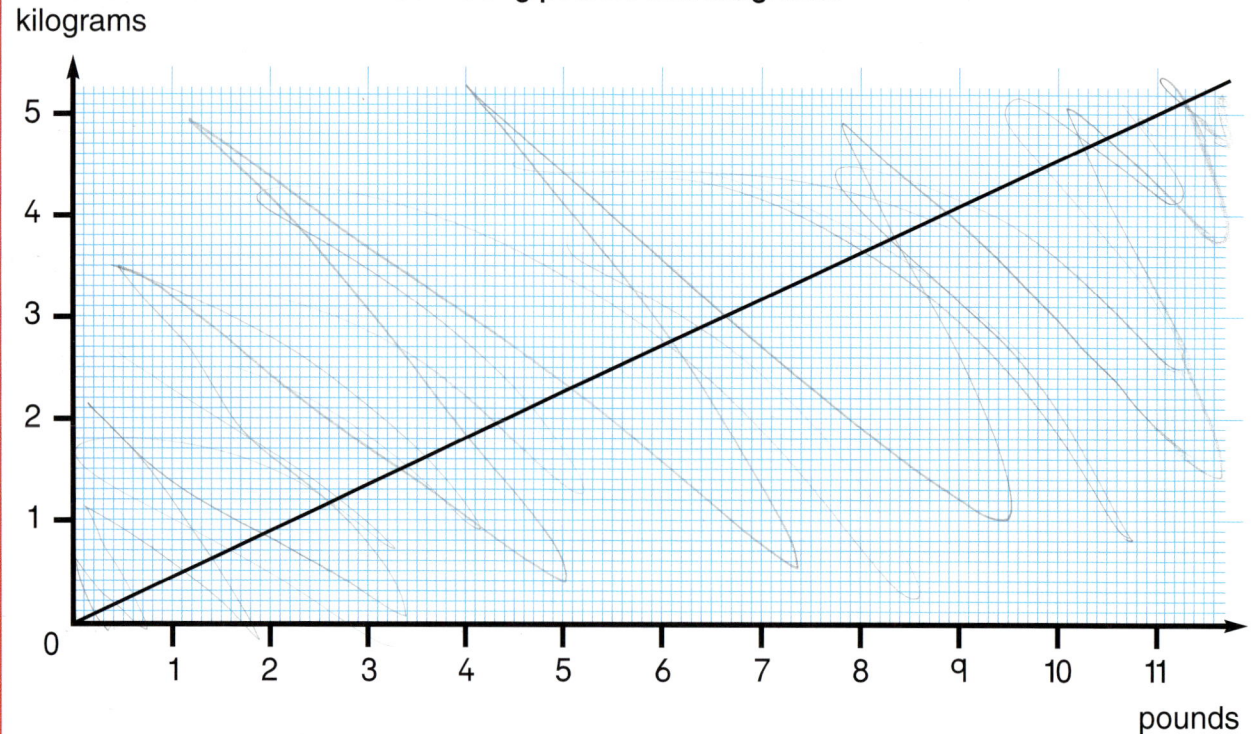

B2 Mrs George made 4 kg of blackberry jam. How many pounds of jam is this?

B3 Roger's granny made 12 jars of strawberry jam. 3 of the jars weighed 1 lb each, 6 of the jars weighed $\frac{1}{2}$ lb each and the other jars weighed 12 oz each.

a How many pounds of jam did she make altogether?

b Give this total in kilograms, rounded to the nearest tenth of a kilogram.

18   M2 Mass

B4 Amrita finds a box of jam. A label says it contains 4.1 kg of jam.

All the jars are identical except one, which is labelled 200 g.

- **a** If there are 13 identical jars, how much do they each weigh in grams?
- **b** How much is this to the nearest ounce?

B5 Megan's favourite jam is raspberry. She finds two 6 oz jars, a 370 g jar, a 1 lb jar and a 580 g jar.

- **a** Roughly how many kilograms of jam is this altogether?
- **b** Which jar is the smallest?

B6 By lunchtime there is twice as much apricot jam left as blackberry jam.

- **a** If there were 4.5 kg of blackberry jam to begin with and $7\frac{1}{2}$ lb of blackberry jam were sold, how many kilograms of apricot jam were left over?
- **b** If there were 3.2 kg of apricot jam to begin with, how many kilograms of apricot jam were sold?

C1
- **a** If an egg weighs roughly 2 oz, find the mass of 1 batch of toffee bars from B1 in pounds.
- **b** By first converting each mass into grams, find the mass of the toffee bars in grams.
- **c** Compare the metric and imperial totals.

C2 Class 6 decides to make 20 batches of toffee bars to sell at the school fair.

- **a** If they want to use metric quantities, how many kilograms of each ingredient will they need?
- **b** Suppose they use the imperial measurements instead, how many pounds and ounces will they need to make 20 batches?
- **c** Compare your answers to questions **a** and **b** for each ingredient.
  What do you notice about the quantities? Which is larger?
- **d** Explain the reason for these differences.
- **e** What problems might this cause?

Key idea	30 g is about an ounce (oz).
	1 kg is about 2.2 pounds (lb).

M2 Mass

M2.4 Reading scales and solving problems

> **Key idea** You can solve problems involving mass.

★1 Give the mass of each parcel in grams.

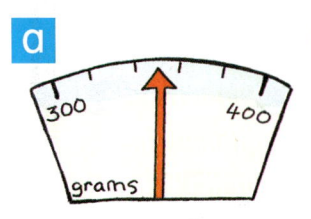

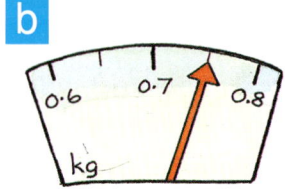

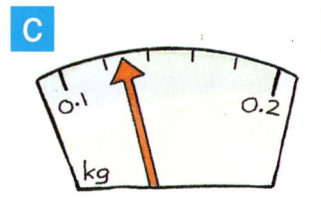

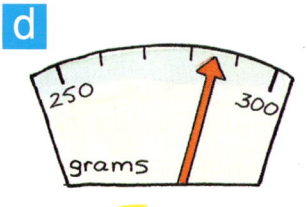

a: 350 grams
b: 0.7 kg
c: 0.15 kg
d: 290 grams

★2 Now give the mass of each parcel in kilograms.

★3 Find the difference in grams between the lightest and heaviest parcels.

★4 Find the total mass in kilograms of all the parcels.

Remember: 1 g = 0.001 kg

A On the planet Zoot they have an unusual postal system.
The currency on the planet Zoot is zogs.

Here is a list of charges in zogs:

Mass not over	Robot Cost in zogs	Railway Cost in zogs	Rocket Cost in zogs
50 g	10	27	40
100 g	16	32	40
150 g	22	37	40
200 g	28	42	40
250 g	34	47	50
300 g	40	52	50
350 g	46	57	50
400 g	52	62	50
500 g	62	69	60
600 g	72	76	60
700 g	82	83	60
800 g	92	90	100
900 g	102	97	100
1000 g	112	104	100
Each extra 250 g or part thereof	Post with mass more than 1000 g cannot be sent by robot	14	25

You have six parcels to send:

[Six scales showing: 45 g, 375 g, 0.9 kg, 0.45 kg, 780 g]

A1 Calculate the cost to send each one by:

- **a** robot post,
- **b** railway post,
- **c** rocket post.

A2 How many zogs would be saved if all the parcels were sent by robot post rather than rocket post?

A3
- **a** What is the total mass of the parcels?
- **b** Work out the cost of posting them all together as one parcel using railway post.
- **c** What is the cost of posting them as one parcel using rocket post?
- **d** For one large parcel, how much more expensive is the rocket post than the railway post?

A4 What is the cheapest way to send:

- **a** a parcel with a mass of 2 lb?
- **b** a parcel with a mass of 9 oz?
- **c** 4 parcels weighing 1 kg each?

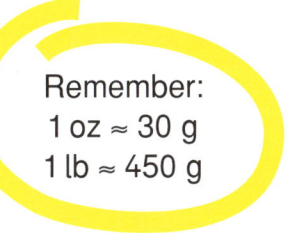

Remember:
1 oz ≈ 30 g
1 lb ≈ 450 g

M2 Mass

Often when we go shopping it can be difficult to work out which is the best buy.

On most supermarket shelves now it tells you the price of an item of food per 100 g or per kg.

B1 Calculate the best buy from each of these food items, by working out the price per 100 g:

a	Choc-chip cookies	50p for 260 g	or	80p for 440 g?
b	Shortbread biscuits	90p for 400 g	or	75p for 300 g?
c	Chocolate bars	576 g for £1.44	or	483 g for £1.38?
d	Cereal	£1.99 for 500 g	or	£1.55 for 375 g?
e	Coffee	£4 for 500 g	or	£3 for 390 g?

B2 You buy all the best buys, what is the total mass of your shopping in kilograms?

B3 There is a special offer on choc-chip cookies.

Which is the best buy now?

SPECIAL OFFER
Three 260g packets for the price of two

B4 If the shop only has 375 g boxes of cereal in stock, how much is this per kilogram?

Are you worth your weight in chocolate?

Fred has won a competition. His prize is his weight in chocolate. He weighs 47 kg. He can choose which type of chocolate he wants for his prize.

Dark Chocolate 400 g — £1.99
Orange Chocolate 100 g — 69p
Mint Chocolate ¼ lb — 73p
Milk Chocolate 1 kg — £4.40
Fruit & nut 1 lb — £2.72
Hazelnut Praline 1 oz — 24p
White chocolate 500 g — £2.75

C1 Work out the price per 100 g of each type of chocolate.

C2 Calculate the value of Fred's prize for each type of chocolate. Answer to the nearest whole pound (£).

C3 Which type of chocolate makes the most valuable prize?

C4 If Fred's brother, who weighs 11 stone 6 lb, had won the competition instead, how much more would the most valuable prize have been worth.

Answer to the nearest whole pound (£).

1 stone = 14 lb
1 lb = 450 g

Key idea You can solve problems involving mass.

M2 Mass

23

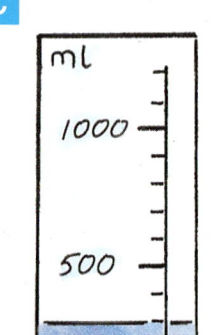

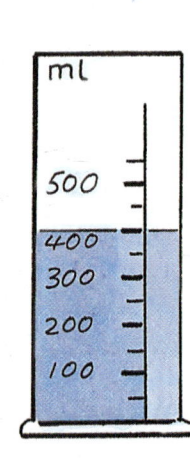

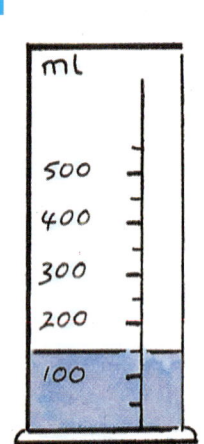

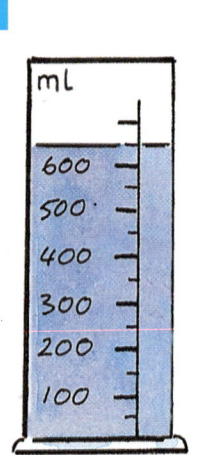

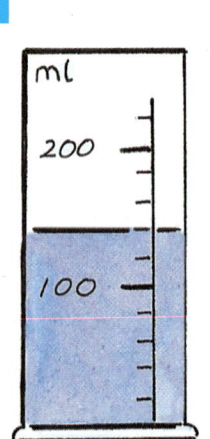

M3.1 Litres and millilitres

> **Key idea** 1 millilitre is one thousandth of 1 litre.

A1 Change these capacities into millilitres.

a 3.550 l   b 4.140 l   c 3.026 l   d 4.819 l

e 2.307 l   f 0.664 l   g 5.079 l   h 7.346 l

A2 How much water in each measuring cylinder? Give your answers in litres.

24   M3 Capacity

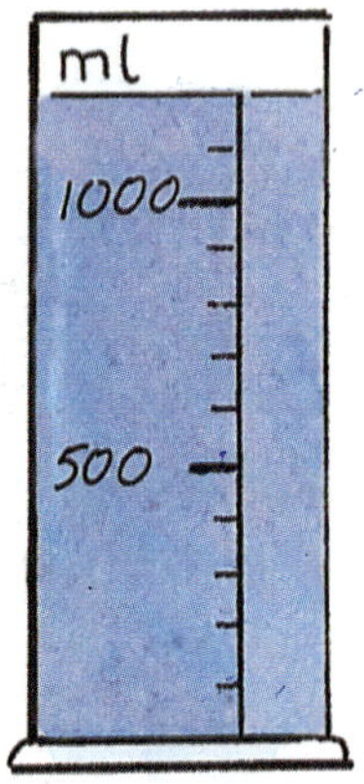

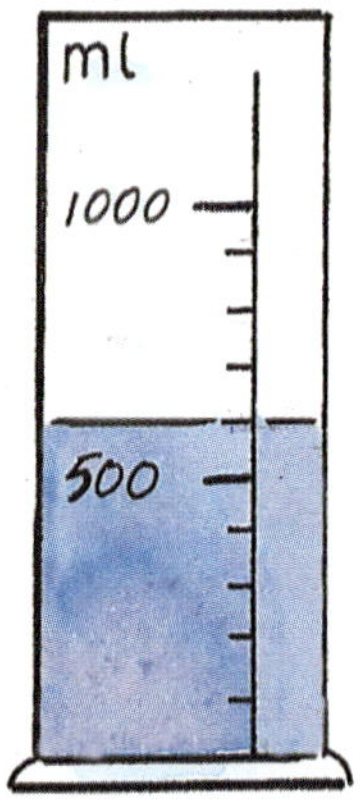

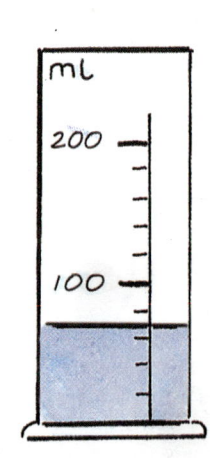

B1 Convert these capacities into litres.

- **a** 150 ml
- **b** 90 ml
- **c** 25 ml
- **d** 64 ml
- **e** 15 ml
- **f** 31 ml
- **g** 4 ml
- **h** 11 ml

B2 Convert these capacities into millilitres.

- **a** 0.321 l
- **b** 0.057 l
- **c** 2.495 l
- **d** 0.006 l
- **e** 0.01 l
- **f** 0.7 l
- **g** 0.402 l
- **h** 0.041 l

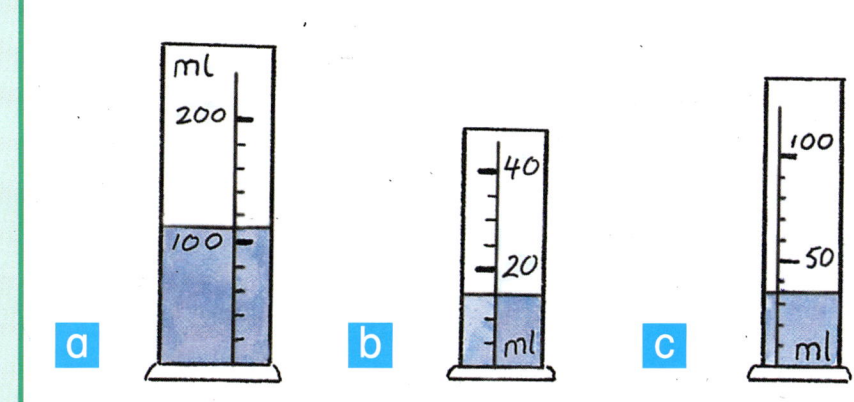

a 100 ml   **b** 20 ml   **c** 50 ml   **d** 10 ml

C1 Give each amount of water in litres.

C2 How many litres altogether?

C3 If I empty one cylinder, what could the total left in litres be? Find all the possibilities.

C4 If I empty 2 cylinders, what could the total left in litres be? Find all the possibilities.

Key idea 1 millilitre is one thousandth of 1 litre.

M3 Capacity

M3.2 Rounding capacity measurements

Key idea	1 litre is 100 centilitres.
	1 centilitre is 10 millilitres.

★1 Give the amount of orange juice in litres.

a 1600 ml   b 800 ml   c 2200 ml   d 1400 ml

e 3300 ml   f 1100 ml   g 500 ml   h 2800 ml

★2 Round your answers to ★1 to the nearest litre.

★3 Do CM 11.

A1 Write in litres how much of each drink was sold.

a 230 cl   b 340 cl   c 190 cl

d 350 cl   e 273 cl   f 138 cl

g 392 cl   h 88 cl

A2 How many centilitres of icecream topping in each bottle?

a 500 ml   b 140 ml   c 330 ml

d 170 ml   e 240 ml   f 166 ml

g 255 ml   h 1040 ml

A3 Peter has plastic bottles of various sizes. Give their capacity rounded to the nearest tenth of a litre.

a 0.68 l   b 0.52 l   c 1.65 l   d 0.97 l

e 0.74 l   f 0.33 l   g 0.41 l   h 2.16 l

M3 Capacity

CM 11

B1 Convert these capacities into centilitres.

a	0.4 l	b	0.75 l	c	0.6 l	d	1.02 l
e	0.08 l	f	4.5 l	g	80 ml	h	69 ml
i	125 ml	j	43 ml	k	364 ml	l	10 ml

B2 Some friends enjoy making homemade lemonade.

Copy and complete the chart showing how much lemonade they made.

centilitres of lemonade made	litres of lemonade to nearest tenth	litres of lemonade to nearest litre
475 cl		
1240 cl		
892 cl		
1158 cl		
661 cl		
927 cl		

C1 How many millilitres of each cough mixture does the chemist have altogether?

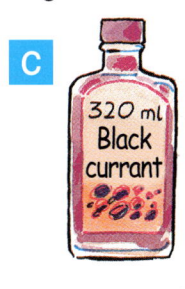

a) 20 cl Honey Mixture
b) 0.26 l Lemon Soother
c) 320 ml Black currant
d) 8.5 cl Strawberry
e) 0.014 l Banana
f) 45 ml Fruity

C2 Give your answers to C1 in centilitres.

C3 Now give your answers in litres to the nearest tenth of a litre.

C4
a) Which cough mixture does the chemist have the most of?
b) Which cough mixture does the chemist have the least of?

C5
a) What is the total number of millilitres of cough mixture of all kinds?
b) Give this total in litres to the nearest tenth of a litre.

Key idea 1 litre is 100 centilitres.
1 centilitre is 10 millilitres.

M3 Capacity

M3.3 Metric and imperial capacities

> **Key idea**
> 4.5 litres is about 1 gallon or 8 pints.
> 1 litre is about $1\frac{3}{4}$ pints.

★1 Which capacity is more:

a) 1 gallon or 2 litres?
b) 6 litres or 2 gallons?
c) 10 litres or 2 gallons?
d) 3 gallons or 20 litres?
e) 16 litres or 4 gallons?
f) 10 gallons or 50 litres?

Remember: 1 pint ≈ 570 ml.

★2 Which capacity is less:

a) 1 pint or 500 ml?
b) 800 ml or 2 pints?
c) 2000 ml or 4 pints?
d) 3 pints or 1800 ml?
e) 10 pints or 6000 ml?
f) 4000 ml or 8 pints?

A1 Change these amounts from gallons to pints.

a) 2 gallons
b) 4 gallons
c) 11 gallons
d) 3 gallons
e) 6 gallons
f) 9 gallons
g) 12 gallons
h) 7 gallons

A2 About how many litres of petrol did these customers buy?

a) 10 gallons
b) 2 gallons
c) 5 gallons
d) 3 gallons
e) 12 gallons
f) 4 gallons
g) 8 gallons
h) 7 gallons

A3 A car has 2 gallons of petrol in it. The petrol tank holds 8 gallons. How many litres of petrol do you need to buy to fill up the tank?

28   M3 Capacity

The paddling pool is empty. To fill it half full takes 70 gallons of water.

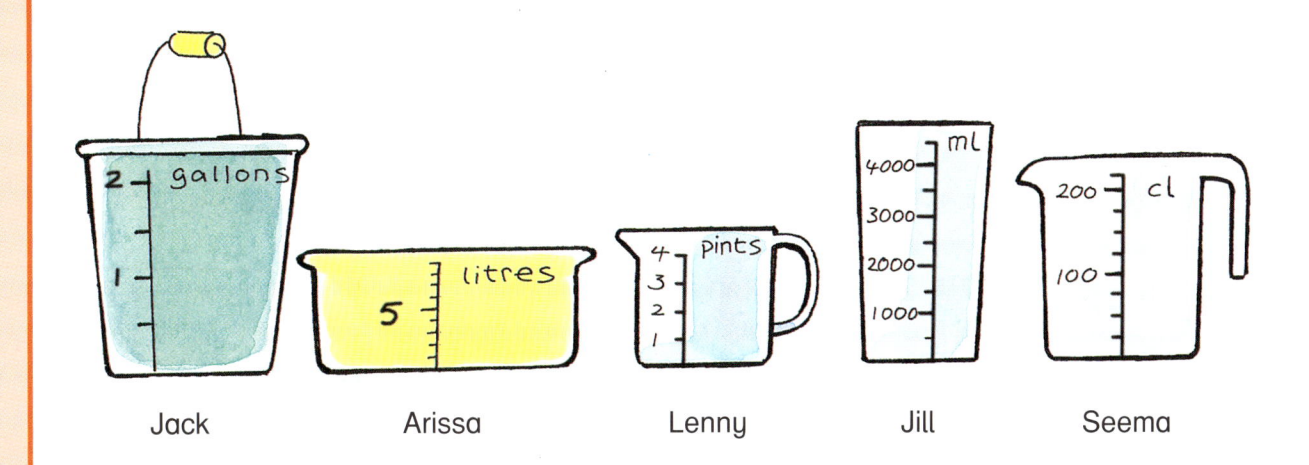

- Jack (bucket, gallons)
- Arissa (litres)
- Lenny (pints)
- Jill (ml)
- Seema (cl)

B1 How many gallons of water would be in the paddling pool if each person poured in 10 containers full of water?

B2
a Jack makes 9 trips with his bucket, Arissa makes 10 trips, Lenny makes 20 trips, Jill makes 15 trips and Seema makes 24 trips.

Work out how many litres of water each one puts into the pool.

b How many litres are in the pool altogether?

c Is the pool more or less than half full? By how much?

C1 You need graph paper and a partner to work with.

Make a graph to convert millilitres to pints. You should be able to convert capacities up to 5000 ml to the nearest quarter of a pint.

Remember to give your graph a title and to label the axes.

C2 Use your graph to convert these capacities to pints.

a 2000 ml **b** 3400 ml **c** 4100 ml **d** 5000 ml

C3 How many millilitres in

a 7 pints? **b** $4\frac{3}{4}$ pints? **c** $8\frac{1}{4}$ pints? **d** $6\frac{1}{2}$ pints?

Key idea 4.5 litres is about 1 gallon or 8 pints.
1 litre is about $1\frac{3}{4}$ pints.

M3 Capacity

M3.4 Capacity problems

| Key idea | You need to be able to read scales accurately and solve real life problems involving capacity. |

★1 Sam has 0.126 litres of cola, Ben has 0.243 litres. How much more has Ben?

★2 Josh drinks a 120 ml glass of orange juice every morning. How much does he drink in a week?

★3 Jane buys a 150 cl bottle of juice. How many 25 cl glasses of juice can she have?

★4 Rachel and Bob wash the car. Rachel uses 1 bucket of water and Bob uses $2\frac{1}{2}$ buckets of water. If the bucket holds 10 pints, how many pints do they use altogether?

A1 A family uses 4 pints of milk every day.

    a How many gallons do they use in a week?

    b How many litres is this?

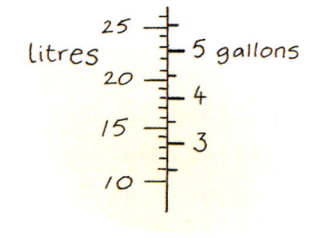

A2 Ramena pours a 333 ml glass of lemonade from a litre bottle. How much lemonade is left in the bottle?

A3 John's water pistol holds 75 cl of water. How many litres does he shoot in total if he refills it and shoots it 6 times?

A4 A school buys 32 pints of milk. Half of this amount is semi-skimmed. How many litres of semi-skimmed are delivered to the school?

A5 Hayley drinks a 0.5 litre bottle of water, a 30 cl bottle of ginger beer and a 125 ml carton of apple juice. How many litres does she drink altogether?

B1 Glen fills his car with 6 gallons of petrol.
He uses a quarter of this amount to get to work.

How many litres does he use?

B2 Jamie's watering can holds 5 pints of water.

How many gallons of water does Jamie use if his garden needs 12 watering cans full of water?

How much is this in litres?

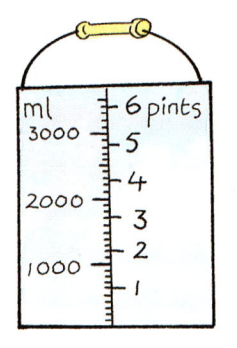

B3 Amy's paddling pool has 15 gallons of water in it.
She adds another 60 litres with the hose pipe and her brother adds 12 buckets of water.

a How many litres are in the pool now?   b How many gallons is this?

B4 Ben has a 2 litre bottle of lemonade. He drinks 40 cl a day and his sister drinks 180 ml a day.

How much is left in the bottle after 3 days?

B5 Cath has 7 litres of petrol. On Monday she buys 9 gallons. She uses 1.5 gallons every day.

How many litres of petrol does she have left when she gets home on Friday?

C1 Craig has a party.

a How many litres of fizzy drinks?   b How many pints of fruit juice?

c How many centilitres of still drinks?   d How many gallons of drinks altogether?

C2 Karl mixes 1 pint of orange juice with $\frac{1}{2}$ litre of ginger beer to make punch.

a How many centilitres of punch does he make?

b How many gallons of these 2 drinks are left?

C3 At the end of the party there is 63 cl of lemonade left, 1 can of cola, $2\frac{1}{2}$ pints of ginger beer and 0.615 l of juice.

a How many pints left over altogether?   b How many gallons were drunk?

M3 Capacity

M4.1 Perimeters of compound shapes

> **Key idea** You find the perimeter of a compound shape by totalling the lengths of all the sides.

★1   Find the perimeter of these shapes:

a

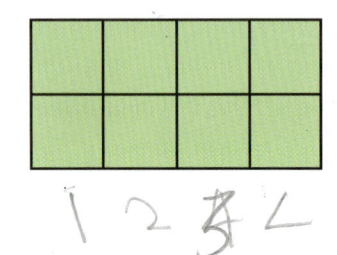

b

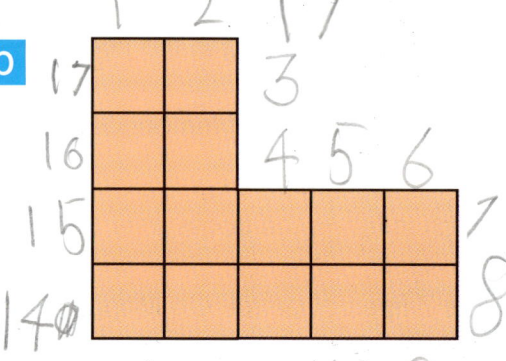

★2   Draw these 4 rectangles in your book.

a   length 5 cm breadth 4 cm

b   length 6 cm breadth 2 cm

c   length 8 cm breadth 3 cm

d   length 6 cm breadth 3 cm

e   Which two rectangles have the same perimeter?

A1   Measure the side of these shapes and find their perimeters.

a

b

c

C1   Sketch as many fish ponds as you can with perimeters of 20 m. Label your sketches to show the length of each side.

M4 Area and perimeter

M4.2 Areas of compound shapes

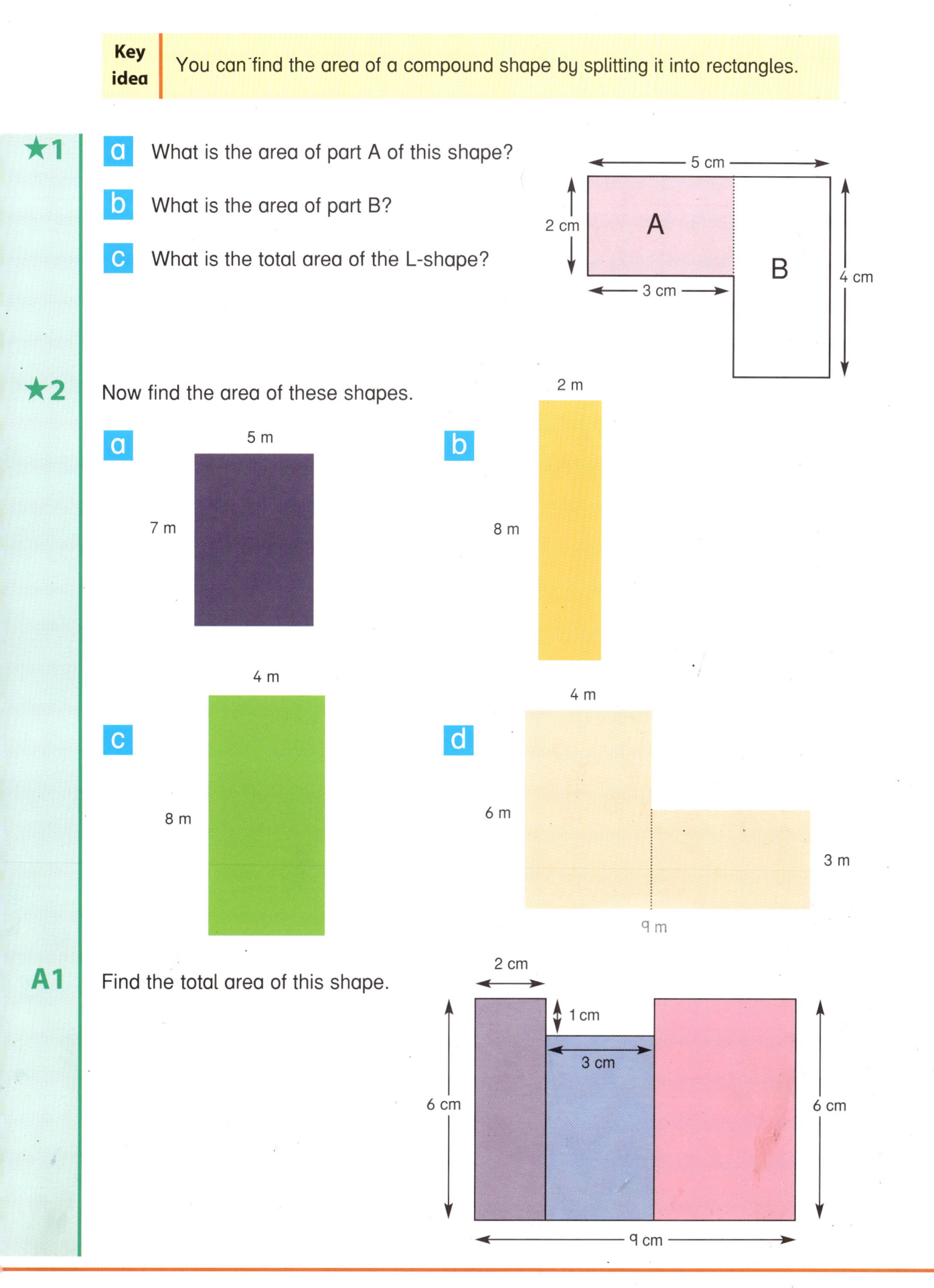

> **Key idea** You can find the area of a compound shape by splitting it into rectangles.

★1
- **a** What is the area of part A of this shape?
- **b** What is the area of part B?
- **c** What is the total area of the L-shape?

★2 Now find the area of these shapes.

a 5 m, 7 m

b 2 m, 8 m

c 4 m, 8 m

d 4 m, 6 m, 3 m, 9 m

A1 Find the total area of this shape.

2 cm, 1 cm, 3 cm, 6 cm, 6 cm, 9 cm

M4 Area and perimeter

33

A2

a. What is the area of the large rectangle?

b. What is the area of part A?

c. What is the area of part B?

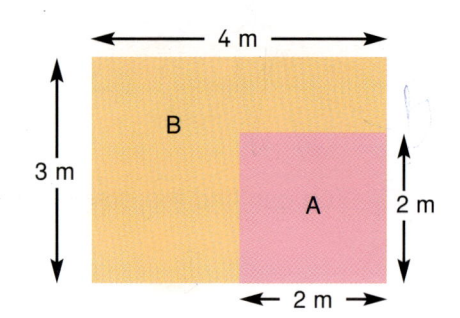

A3 See if you can use the same method as you did in A2 to find the area of the shaded part of this shape.

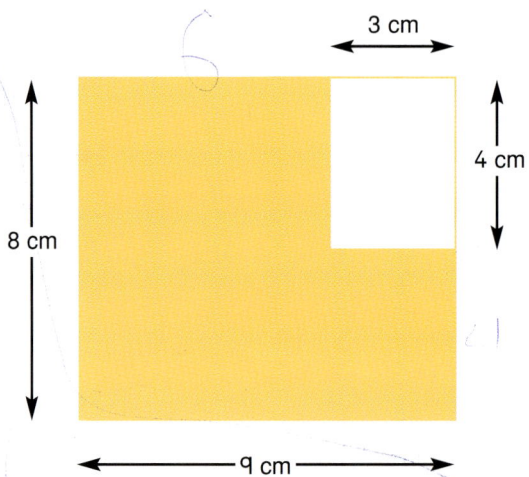

A4 Find the total area of this shape.

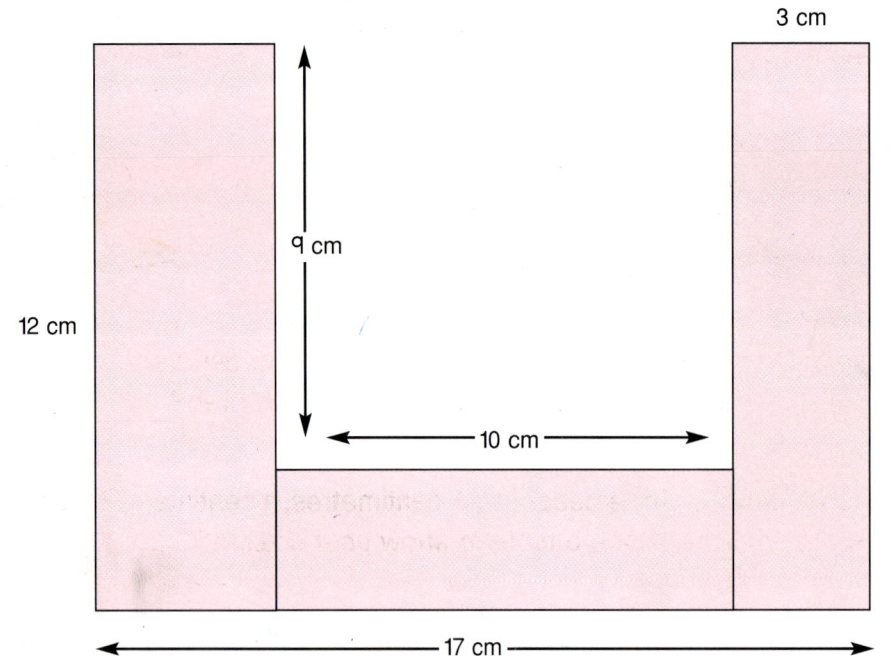

C1 Draw as many shapes as you can with an area of 24 cm².

All of their corners must be right-angled.

Use factors.

Key idea You can find the area of a compound shape by splitting it into rectangles.

M4 Area and perimeter

M4.3 Surface areas

> **Key idea** If you know the dimensions of a cuboid you can find its surface area.

★1 You need interlocking cubes.

Make a table showing the surface area of sticks made of 1, 2, 3, ... 10 cubes.

Number of cubes	Surface area
1	6 cm²
2	10 cm²

A1 You need interlocking cubes.

a Imagine a cuboid like this, made of centimetre cubes.

It has breadth 1 cm, length 2 cm, height 1 cm.

What is its surface area?

Predict: Will doubling the number of cubes like this double the surface area?

b Now make the shape with breadth 2 cm, length 2 cm, height 1 cm.

c Was your prediction correct? Explain.

A2 Now extend the cuboid by one more centimetre so that it measures breadth 2 cm, length 3 cm, height 1 cm. What is the surface area?

A3 Keep extending the length of the cuboid to 6 centimetres, 1 centimetre at a time, and calculating the area each time. Make a table to show your calculations.

Length	Breadth	Height	Surface area
1 cm	2 cm	1 cm	
2 cm	2 cm	1 cm	
3 cm	2 cm	1 cm	

What patterns do you notice?

M4 Area and perimeter

B1 Imagine a cube. Its sides measure 1 cm.

What is the surface area?

B2 Imagine a cube with sides of 2 cm.

The length of each side has been doubled.
Will the surface area be doubled? Predict.

You need interlocking cubes.

B3 Make the cube from B2.

Was your prediction right? Why?

B4 Continue the pattern in a table showing the length and surface area of the cubes with sides 1 cm, 2 cm, 3 cm, ... 10 cm.

B5 a Can you spot any pattern in your results?

b Can you predict the surface area of the next size cube?

C1 You need interlocking cubes.

What happens to the surface area as you grow other shapes?

You could try something like this or you might prefer to try a shape of your own.

Record your results and describe any patterns you notice.

Key idea If you know the dimensions of a cuboid you can find its surface area.

M4 Area and perimeter

M 4.4 Areas of isosceles triangles

Key idea | When you split a square into 2 triangles, the area of each triangle is half the area of the square.

★1 Use dotty paper.

Make a square with sides of 6 centimetres. Make a diagonal and then find the area of the square and the triangle.

A1
a What is the area of this square?

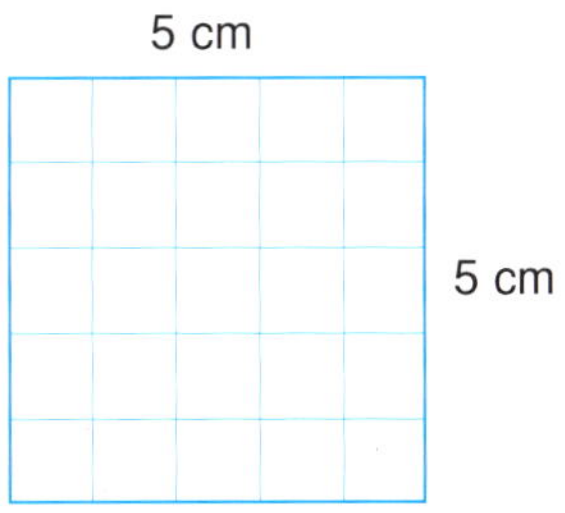

5 cm
5 cm

b What is the area of the shaded triangle?

5 cm
5 cm

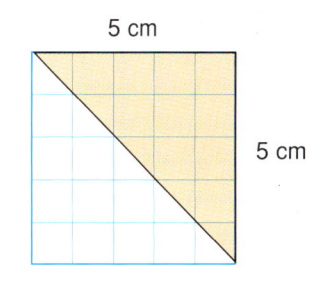

A2
a What is the area of the square?

b What is the area of the shaded triangle?

10 cm
10 cm

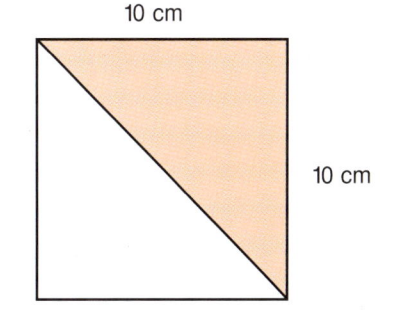

A3 What is the area of the triangle?

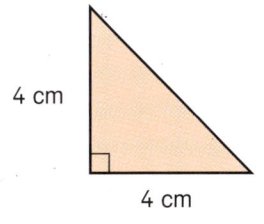

4 cm
4 cm

B1 Find the areas of the shapes by dividing them into squares and isosceles triangles.

a 4 cm, 8 cm

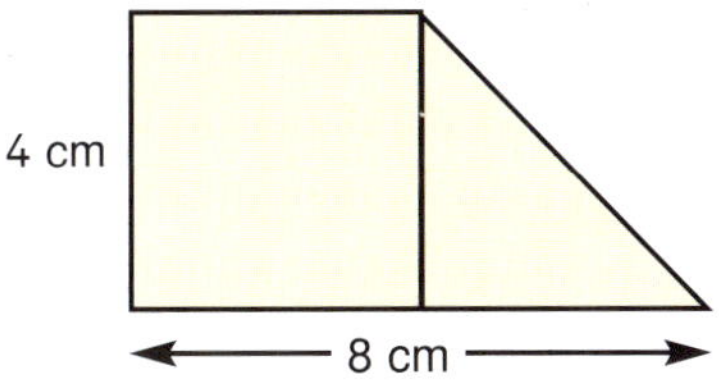

b 3 cm, 6 cm

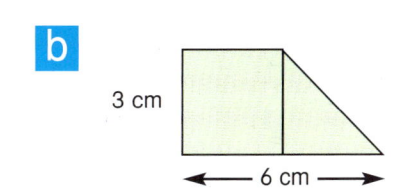

c 9 m, 18 m

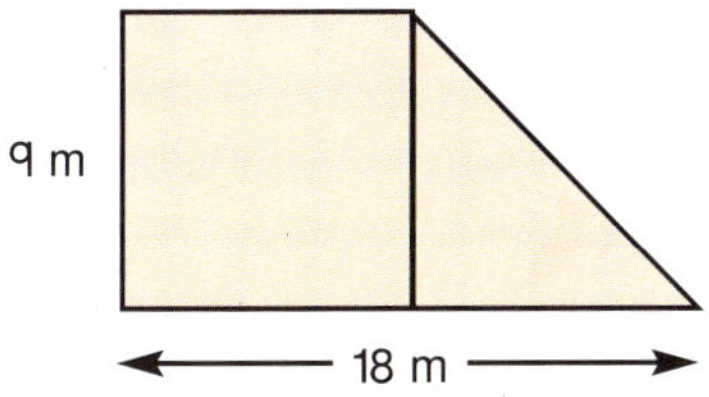

d 5 cm, 5 cm

M4 Area and perimeter

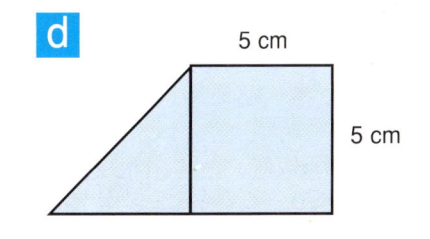

C1   *Use dotty paper.*

Investigate what happens to areas you enclose as you join 6, 7 or 8 neighbouring points.

Both of these shapes have 8 neighbouring points on their border.

a   What shapes can you make?

b   What area does each shape cover?

c   What difference does it make to your findings if there are some points inside your shape compared with when there are no points inside?

> **Key idea**   When you split a square into 2 triangles, the area of each triangle is half the area of the square.

M4.5 Area of right-angled triangles

> **Key idea** Halving the area of a rectangle gives the area of a triangle.

A1 Calculate the area of these rectangles, then the area of the shaded triangles.

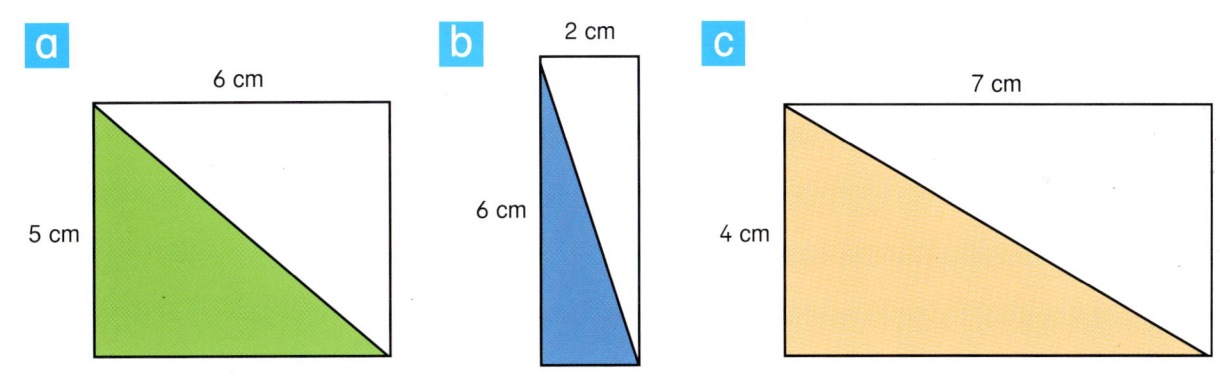

a) 6 cm × 5 cm

b) 2 cm × 6 cm

c) 7 cm × 4 cm

A2 Now find the area of these triangles.

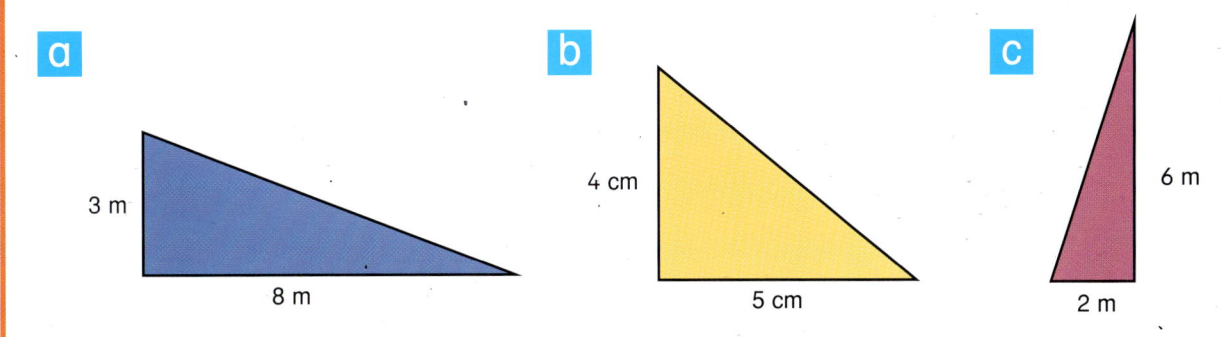

a) 3 m, 8 m

b) 4 cm, 5 cm

c) 6 m, 2 m

A3 These shapes are divided into triangles and rectangles. Find their areas.

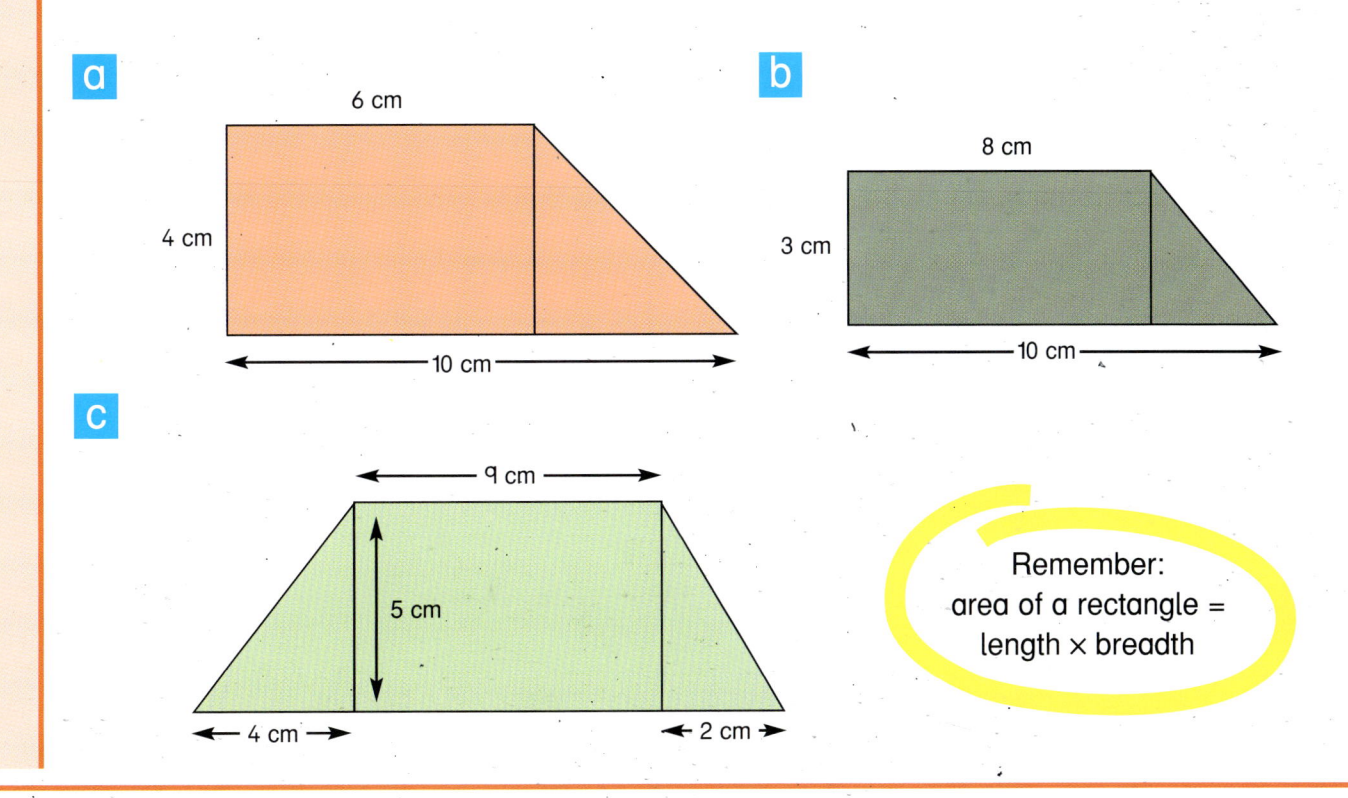

a) 6 cm (top), 4 cm (side), 10 cm (bottom)

b) 8 cm (top), 3 cm (side), 10 cm (bottom)

c) 9 cm (top), 5 cm (height), 4 cm and 2 cm (bottom extensions)

Remember:
area of a rectangle = length × breadth

M4 Area and perimeter

B1 Work out the area of this shape.

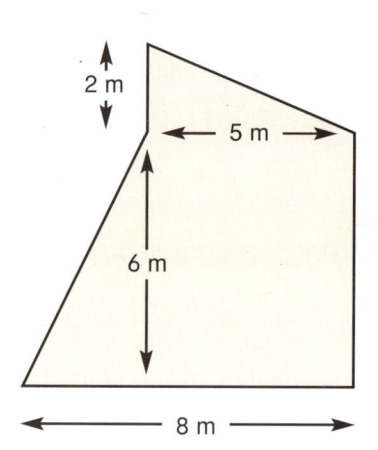

B2 Find the area of this shape.

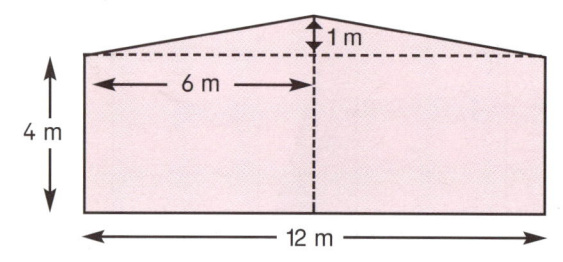

B3 Now find the area of this shape using the 'missing' triangle.

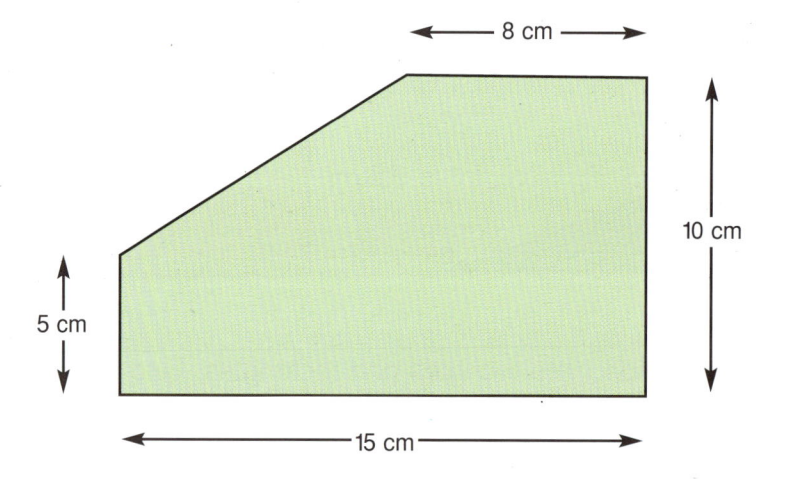

C1 A hexagonal climbing frame stands in the rectangular area shown. The hexagonal area will be filled with bark and the rest covered with turf.

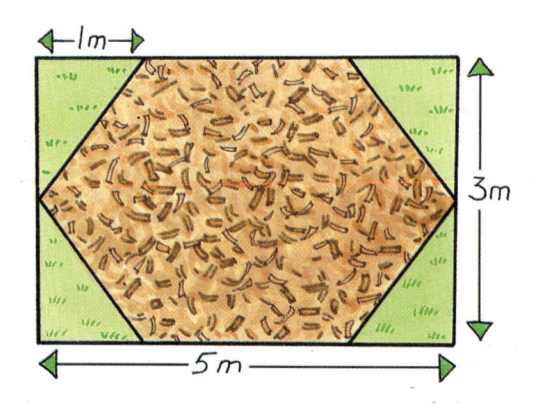

a How many square metres of turf will be needed?

b How many square metres will be covered by bark?

| Key idea | Halving the area of a rectangle gives the area of a triangle. |

M4 Area and perimeter

M5.1 World time zones

> **Key idea** The time in all places in a particular time zone is the same.

You need CM 15.

A1 If it is 12:00 GMT at the Prime Meridian, what time is it in

- a New York?
- b Rome?
- c Perth?
- d Los Angeles?
- e Oslo?
- f Tokyo?

A2 If it is 09:00 GMT in London, what is the time in

- a Johannesburg?
- b Karachi?
- c Sydney?
- d Rio de Janeiro?
- e Los Angeles?
- f Lima?

A3 If it is 18:00 GMT in Britain, what is the time in

- a Karachi?
- b Johannesburg?
- c Rome?
- d New York?
- e San Francisco?
- f Rio de Janeiro?

B1 It is 19:00 GMT at the Prime Meridian. What time is it in

- a Lima?
- b Fairbanks?
- c Karachi?

Remember some countries choose their own time.

B2 It is 15:00 GMT in the United Kingdom. What is the time in

- a Paris?
- b Moscow?
- c Beijing?

B3 My flight to New York leaves London Heathrow at 16:05. If the flight takes 7 hours 40 min, what will the time be in New York when I arrive?

B4 Jamie rings a friend in Australia who complains because it is almost midnight there.
If it is 23:45 in Perth, what is the time in England?

M5 Time   CM 15   41

B5 It is 10 a.m. on Saturday in Hong Kong. Salmi wants to ring her friend in Britain.

a What time is it in Britain when it is 10 a.m. in Hong Kong?

b When it is 10 a.m. in Britain, what time will it be in Hong Kong?

c Suggest a sensible time for Salmi to ring her friend.
Give the times in both countries.

Key idea The time in all places in a particular time zone is the same.

M5.2 | **Time zones and date changes**

> **Key idea** | When it is noon in Britain it is still morning in Canada, but it is already evening in India.

You need CM 15.

1 If it is 10 a.m. GMT in London, what time is it in

   a Tokyo?   **b** Rome?   **c** Rio de Janeiro?

   d Nordvik?   **e** Beijing?

2 It is 11:25 p.m. in New York. Find another city on the map where the time will be the same.

3 Find 5 pairs of cities which have a 2 hour time difference between them.

4 Here is part of a Eurostar timetable.
Departure times from Waterloo are shown in GMT.
Arrival times in Paris are shown in local time.

The journey time is 3 hours.

Departs London Waterloo	Arrives Paris Nord
05:15	
	10:59
07:23	11:23
	12:43

   a Explain why the 07:23 departure appears to take 4 hours.

   b Copy and complete the timetable.

5 The President of the USA needs to contact other world leaders. He would like to speak to each one at 15:00 local time in their own country.

If he telephones from the New York time zone, what time should he choose to ring

   a London?   **b** Paris?   **c** Tokyo?   **d** Mexico City?

6 Here is part of a timetable showing flights from London to New York. Departure times are given in GMT and arrival times are local.

Departs London, Heathrow	Arrives New York, John F Kennedy
08:45	11:25
11:05	13:45
13:30	
	18:45
18:05	
	22:45

All flights take the same length of time.

a How long does the journey last?

b Copy and complete the timetable.

7 If it is 22:00 or 10 p.m. in London on Friday 20th July, what will the time and date be in

a Moscow?   **b** Sydney?   **c** Santiago?

8 A detective in San Francisco needs to speak to a colleague in Rome.

If it is 23:30 or 11:30 p.m. on Tuesday 7th August in San Francisco, what will the time and date be in Rome?

9 A business woman flies from Johannesburg to Sydney.

Her flight departs at 18:10 on Wednesday 20 June and takes 12 hours.

When will she land in Sydney?

> **Key idea** When it is noon in Britain it is still morning in Canada, but it is already evening in India.

M5.3 Solving time problems

> **Key idea** To change seconds to minutes or minutes to hours use grouping in 60s.

★1 Look at the opening times for the swimming pool.

	a.m.		p.m.
Sunday	9:00	to	6:00
Monday	10:00	to	7:00
Tuesday	10:00	to	7:00
Wednesday		Closed	
Thursday	9:30	to	7:00
Friday	9:30	to	8:30
Saturday	7:00	to	6:00

a How many hours is the pool open on Monday?

b Which day has the earliest opening time?

c Andre arrives at 9:35 a.m. on Tuesday. How many minutes must he wait for the pool to open?

d Shana arrives at 4:50 p.m. on Saturday. How long before the pool closes?

A1 Find **a** 4 hours 28 minutes × 3   **b** 7 minutes 40 seconds × 4

A2 Here is part of a bus timetable:

Ryde	15:40
Sandown	16:10
Shanklin	16:25
Ventnor	16:42
Blackgang	17:12
Freshwater	17:40
Yarmouth	18:08

a How long does the bus take to travel from Ryde to Ventnor?

b Sammi wants to get on the bus at Blackgang. He reaches the stop at 4:55 p.m. How long does he have to wait for the bus to arrive?

c Keri travels from Ventnor to Yarmouth. How long does her journey take?

d How long does it take for the bus to travel from Ryde to Yarmouth?

e Write the timetable using 12-hour clock times.

B1 Seb plans to cook a chicken.

The instructions tell him to cook it for 50 minutes per kilogram.

   a If the chicken has a mass of 1.5 kg, how long must he cook it for?

   b If he wants it to be ready at 12:45, when should he put it into the oven?

B2 Terry and Habib complete the first stage of the rally in 2 hours 45 minutes.

   a If they cross the finish line at 10:25, what time did they start?

   b The second stage takes them 3 times as long.

      How many hours and minutes does the second stage take?

   c What is their total time over the 2 stages?

B3 A swimathon is held to raise money for charity.

   a Chris swims 32 lengths. His average time for a length is 40 seconds.

      How many minutes and seconds does he swim for?

   b Roseena completes 5 lengths in a time of 8 minutes 40 seconds.

      At this rate how long would it take to complete 15 lengths?

   c The local film crew spend 80 minutes at the event.

      If they leave at 12:35, when did they arrive?

C1 Make up some word problems involving time for a friend to solve.

Key idea | To change seconds to minutes or minutes to hours use grouping in 60s.

M5 Time

SS1.1 Parallelograms and rhombuses

Key idea	A parallelogram is a quadrilateral with opposite sides parallel. A rhombus is a parallelogram with 4 equal sides.

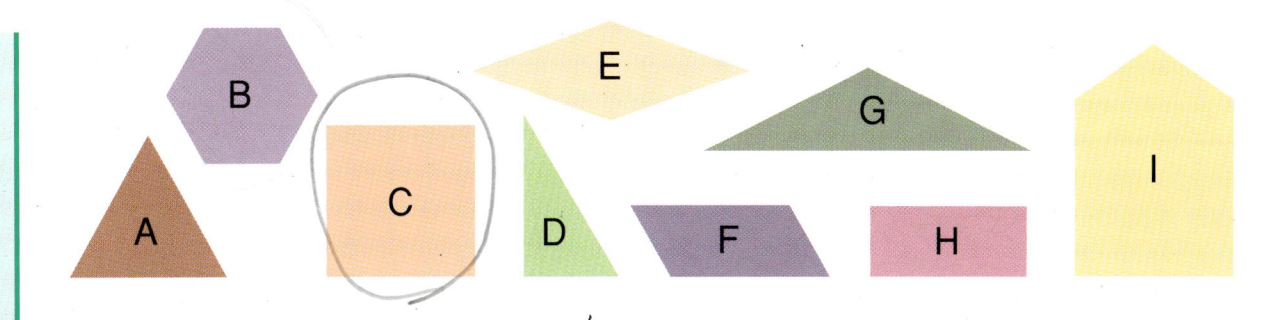

★1 a In which of these shapes is every side equal?

   b Which of these shapes has no sides equal?

★2 a In which of these shapes is every angle a right angle?

   b Which of these shapes have no right angles?

★3 a In which of these shapes is every side parallel to another side?

   b Which of these shapes has no parallel sides?

A1 Look at the shapes above.

   a Which of these shapes are not quadrilaterals?

   b Which shape is a parallelogram?

   c Which shape is a rhombus?

A2 Do CM 16.

B1 I am thinking of a quadrilateral. What could it be?

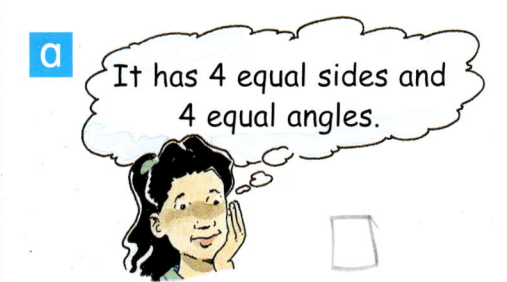

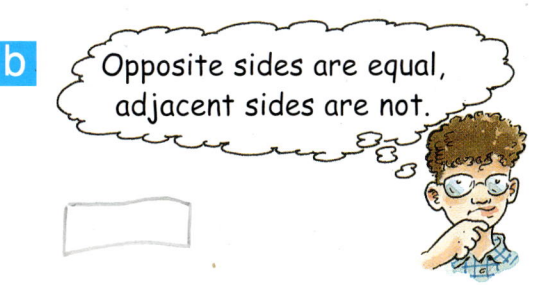

   a It has 4 equal sides and 4 equal angles.

   b Opposite sides are equal, adjacent sides are not.

SS1 Properties of 2-D shapes

c *It has 2 obtuse angles and 4 equal sides.*

d *It has 4 equal angles, but all sides are not equal.*

B2 Do CM 17.

C1

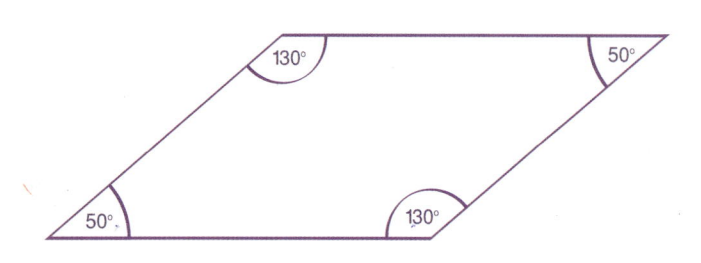

Adjacent angles are next to each other.

Look at the parallelogram above.

a What do you notice about opposite angles?

b Now look at 2 adjacent angles. Add them together. What is the total?

c Look at other pairs of adjacent angles. What are their totals?

d What can you say about adjacent angles of this parallelogram?

C2 Look at the angles on CM 17.

a What do you notice about opposite angles?

b Look at pairs of adjacent angles. What are their totals?

c What can you say about adjacent angles of these parallelograms?

C3

a If a parallelogram has one angle of 40°, work out what the other 3 angles must be.

b If you draw a parallelogram with one angle 105°, how big do you think the other angles will be?

> **Key idea**
> A parallelogram is a quadrilateral with opposite sides parallel.
> A rhombus is a parallelogram with 4 equal sides.

48   SS1 Properties of 2-D shapes   CM 17

SS1.2 Trapeziums and kites

> **Key idea** | A trapezium is a quadrilateral with only 1 pair of parallel sides. A kite is a quadrilateral with 2 pairs of adjacent sides equal and each angle less than 180°.

★1 Work in a group.

You need shape cards from CM 20.

Play 'Property pairs':

- Place the cards face down on the table.
- Take turns to try and make a pair.
- The first player chooses 2 cards and turns them face upwards.
- They score 1 point if they can make a pair by giving a property shared by both shapes.
- Any player can then score a bonus point by suggesting a different property which also makes a pair.
- At the end of each turn, put the cards face down again ready for the next player to choose 2 different cards.
- The winner is the player with the most points after 5 goes each.

SS1 Properties of 2-D shapes

B1 You need an equilateral triangle.
Work with a partner.

You may draw round an equilateral triangle up to 4 times.

a Find all the quadrilaterals you can make.

Draw and name them.

b Name the quadrilaterals that cannot be made.

c Look at the angles and lengths of sides and explain why you cannot make these quadrilaterals.

B2 Repeat B1 using a scalene triangle.

B3 Repeat B1 using a right-angled isoceles triangle.

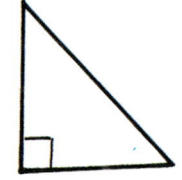

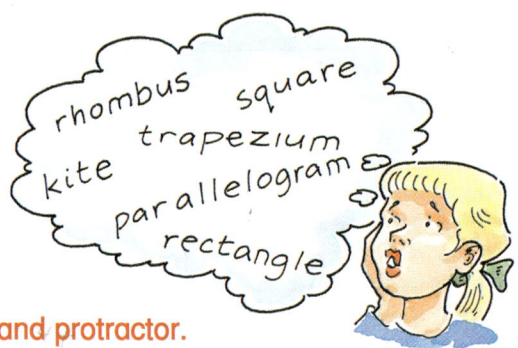

rhombus square trapezium kite parallelogram rectangle

C1 You need a ruler and protractor.

I am thinking of a special quadrilateral. Use your ruler and protractor to draw as many possibilities as you can.

a All the sides are 5 cm.

b The angles are 15°, 15°, 165° and 165°.

c The sides are 4 cm, 4 cm, 6 cm and 6 cm.

d The angles are 110°, 110°, 90° and 50°.

Key idea A trapezium is a quadrilateral with only 1 pair of parallel sides. A kite is a quadrilateral with 2 pairs of adjacent sides equal and each angle less than 180°.

SS1 Properties of 2-D shapes

SS1.3 Diagonals

| Key idea | The diagonals of some quadrilaterals intersect at right angles. The diagonals of some quadrilaterals bisect one another. |

★1 **Work with a partner.**

Which of these drawing do not show diagonals?

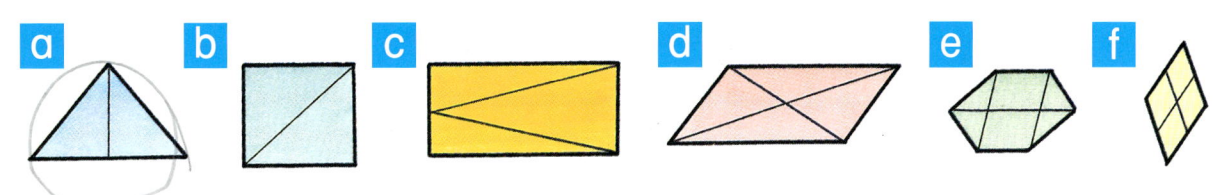

a b c d e f

★2 In which pairs of lines does the short line bisect the longer line?

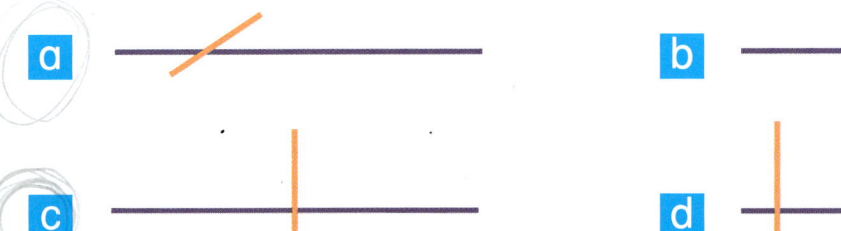

a   b

c   d

e   f

★3 In which pairs of lines does the longer line bisect the shorter line?

★4 In which pair of lines do both lines bisect each other?

★5 In which pairs of lines do both lines intersect at right angles?

A1 Do CM 23.

A2

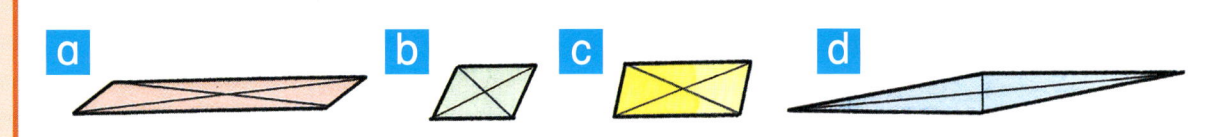

a b c d

a Look at these parallelograms. What can you say about all their diagonals?

b Is this true for any parallelogram? Can you find an exception?

SS1 Properties of 2-D shapes

B1 **a**

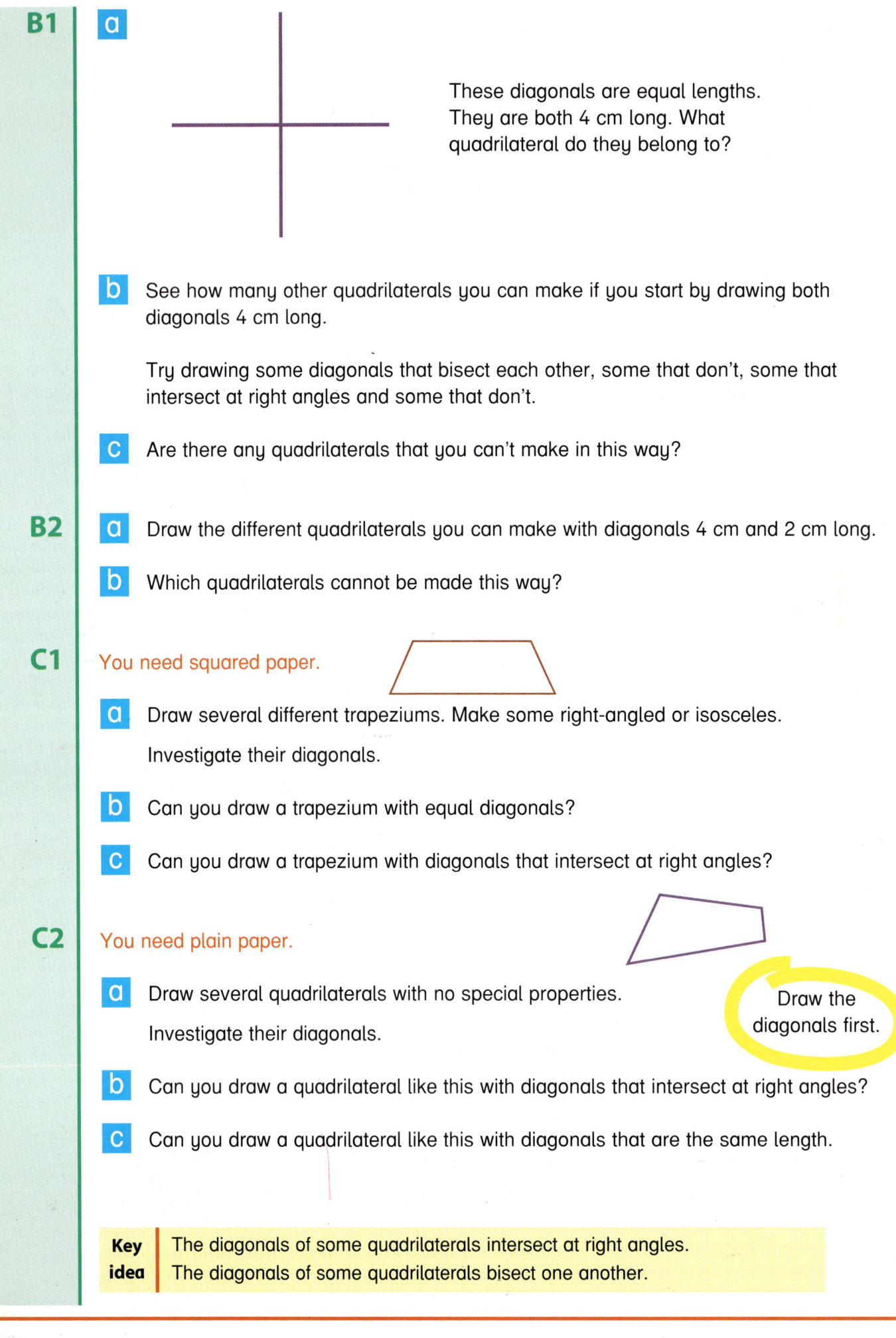

These diagonals are equal lengths. They are both 4 cm long. What quadrilateral do they belong to?

b See how many other quadrilaterals you can make if you start by drawing both diagonals 4 cm long.

Try drawing some diagonals that bisect each other, some that don't, some that intersect at right angles and some that don't.

c Are there any quadrilaterals that you can't make in this way?

B2 **a** Draw the different quadrilaterals you can make with diagonals 4 cm and 2 cm long.

b Which quadrilaterals cannot be made this way?

C1 You need squared paper.

a Draw several different trapeziums. Make some right-angled or isosceles.
Investigate their diagonals.

b Can you draw a trapezium with equal diagonals?

c Can you draw a trapezium with diagonals that intersect at right angles?

C2 You need plain paper.

a Draw several quadrilaterals with no special properties.
Investigate their diagonals.

Draw the diagonals first.

b Can you draw a quadrilateral like this with diagonals that intersect at right angles?

c Can you draw a quadrilateral like this with diagonals that are the same length.

| Key idea | The diagonals of some quadrilaterals intersect at right angles. The diagonals of some quadrilaterals bisect one another. |

SS1 Properties of 2-D shapes

SS1.4 Circles

> **Key idea**
> Concentric circles have a common centre.
> An arc is any part of the circumference of a circle.

1 **You need a pair of compasses.**

Practise drawing some circles with a pair of compasses, then try drawing the pattern:

- **a** Draw a circle in the centre of a page with radius 4 cm.
  Keep the radius at 4 cm every time you draw a circle on the pattern.

- **b** Mark a point on the circumference of the circle to use as the centre of another circle. Draw a circle.

- **c** Use one of the points of intersection with the first circle as a new centre and draw another circle.

- **d** Keep going until you have drawn 6 new circles.

- **e** Now draw concentric circles with a radius a little bit less than 4 cm.

- **f** Draw some concentric circles around the whole design.

2 Explore what happens if you make the radius of the central circle 4 cm but choose a smaller or larger radius for the other circles.

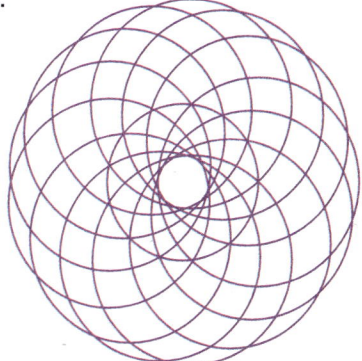

SS1 Properties of 2-D shapes

SS1.5 Tangrams

> **Key idea** A tangram is made from pieces cut from a single square.

1   You need your tangram.

With the 2 small triangles, make and draw

|a| a square |b| a triangle |c| a parallelogram.

2   With the 2 small triangles and the square, make and draw

|a| a rectangle |b| a triangle |c| a parallelogram.

3   With the 2 small triangles and the parallelogram, make and draw

|a| a rectangle |b| a triangle |c| a parallelogram.

4   With the 2 small triangles and the middle-sized triangle, make and draw

|a| a rectangle |b| a triangle |c| a parallelogram.

5   Use 4 tangram pieces to make each of these shapes.

|a| 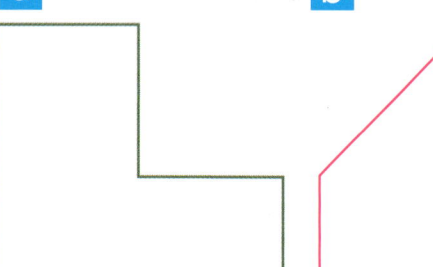 |b| 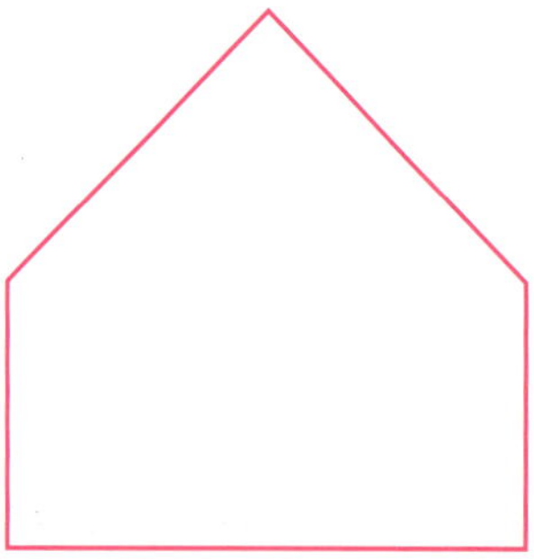 |c|

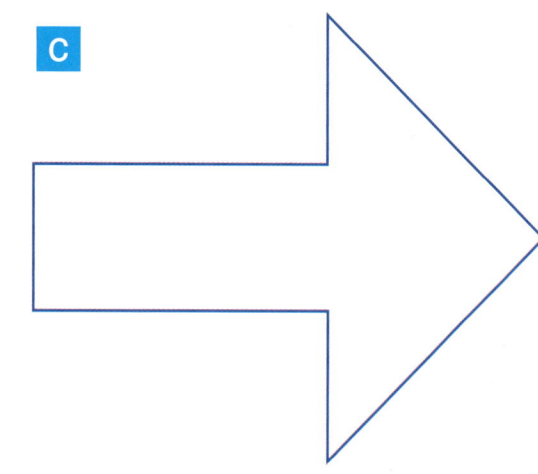

6   Using all 7 tangram pieces make and draw

|a| a rectangle |b| a triangle |c| a parallelogram.

7   Find as many ways as you can to make a trapezium.

Can you make a trapezium using 2 tangram pieces?

3 tangram pieces?   4 tangram pieces?   5 tangram pieces?
6 tangram pieces?   7 tangram pieces?

SS1 Properties of 2-D shapes

SS1.6 Reasoning about shapes

> **Key idea** You can check a general statement by looking for examples that do not satisfy it.

A1 Work with a partner. You need CM 26.

Copy and complete this Carroll diagram for quadrilaterals.

	Has every side equal	Does not have every side equal
Has every angle equal		
Does not have every angle equal		

A2 Investigate the general statement:

All quadrilaterals with every side equal also have every angle equal.

a Can you find a quadrilateral with every side equal which does not have every angle equal?

b Do you think this general statement is true or false?

A3 **a** Make a general statement about quadrilaterals with every side equal for your partner to test. Try to find one you think is true.

b Investigate your partner's statement. Do you think it is true or false?

SS1 Properties of 2-D shapes

B1

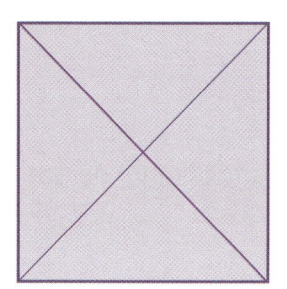

A square has opposite sides equal and diagonals which bisect each other.

a Which other quadrilaterals also have both of these 2 properties?

b Investigate the general statement: 'Quadrilaterals with opposite sides equal have diagonals that bisect each other'. Draw a Carroll diagram to help you.

c Do you think this statement is always true?

B2

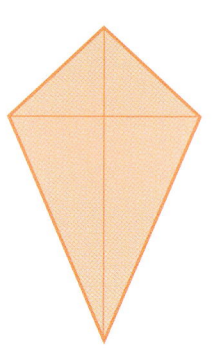

A kite has 2 pairs of adjacent sides equal and diagonals which intersect at right angles.

a Make a general statement about quadrilaterals that have adjacent sides equal.

b Investigate your statement and see if you can find examples that satisfy it.

c Can you find a general statement about quadrilaterals with adjacent sides equal that you think is always true?

C1 Investigate quadrilaterals which have 2 pairs of equal sides.

a Make and test general statements about quadrilaterals that have 2 pairs of equal sides. Draw Carroll diagrams to help you.

Say if you think the statements are true or false.

b Find a general statement about quadrilaterals with 2 pairs of equal sides which you think is true.

What can you say about the angles or the diagonals?

Key idea	You can check a general statement by looking for examples that do not satisfy it.

SS1 Properties of 2-D shapes

SS2.1 Properties of 3-D shapes

| Key idea | A regular dodecahedron is a polyhedron with 12 faces that are regular pentagons. |

★1 a   b   c   d

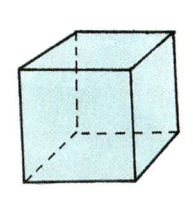

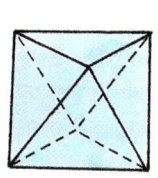

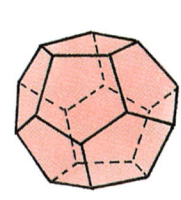

Copy and complete this table.

Name of shape	Number of edges meeting at each vertex
a	
b	
c	
d	

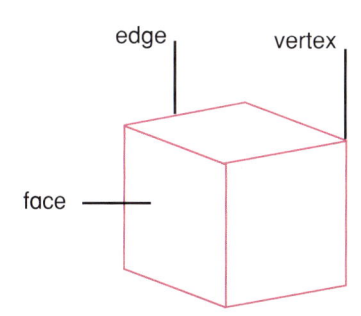

★2 You need interlocking tiles.

Make a tetrahedron.

B1

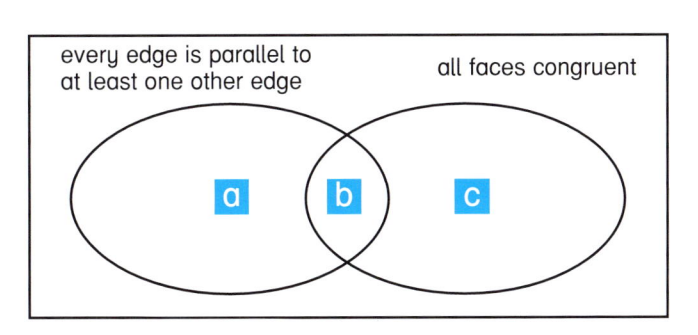

every edge is parallel to at least one other edge   all faces congruent

a   b   c

Name polyhedra that belong in each section.

B2

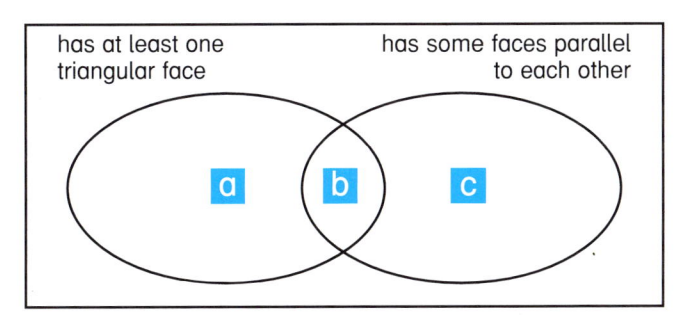

has at least one triangular face   has some faces parallel to each other

a   b   c

Name polyhedra that belong in each section.

SS2 Properties of 3-D shapes   57

SS2.2 Nets for closed cubes

> **Key idea** | Some hexominoes are nets and will form a closed cube.

★1 You need 6 interlocking square tiles.

Use interlocking square tiles to make hexominoes and see if they are nets of a cube.

How many different nets can you find?

A1 This hexomino is not a net of a cube.

Draw another hexomino which is not the net of a cube.

A2 Which of these hexominoes are the nets of a cube?

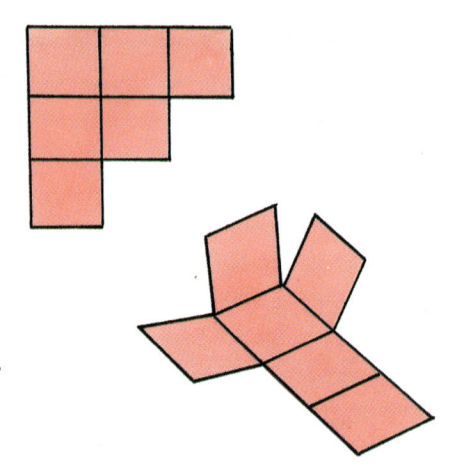

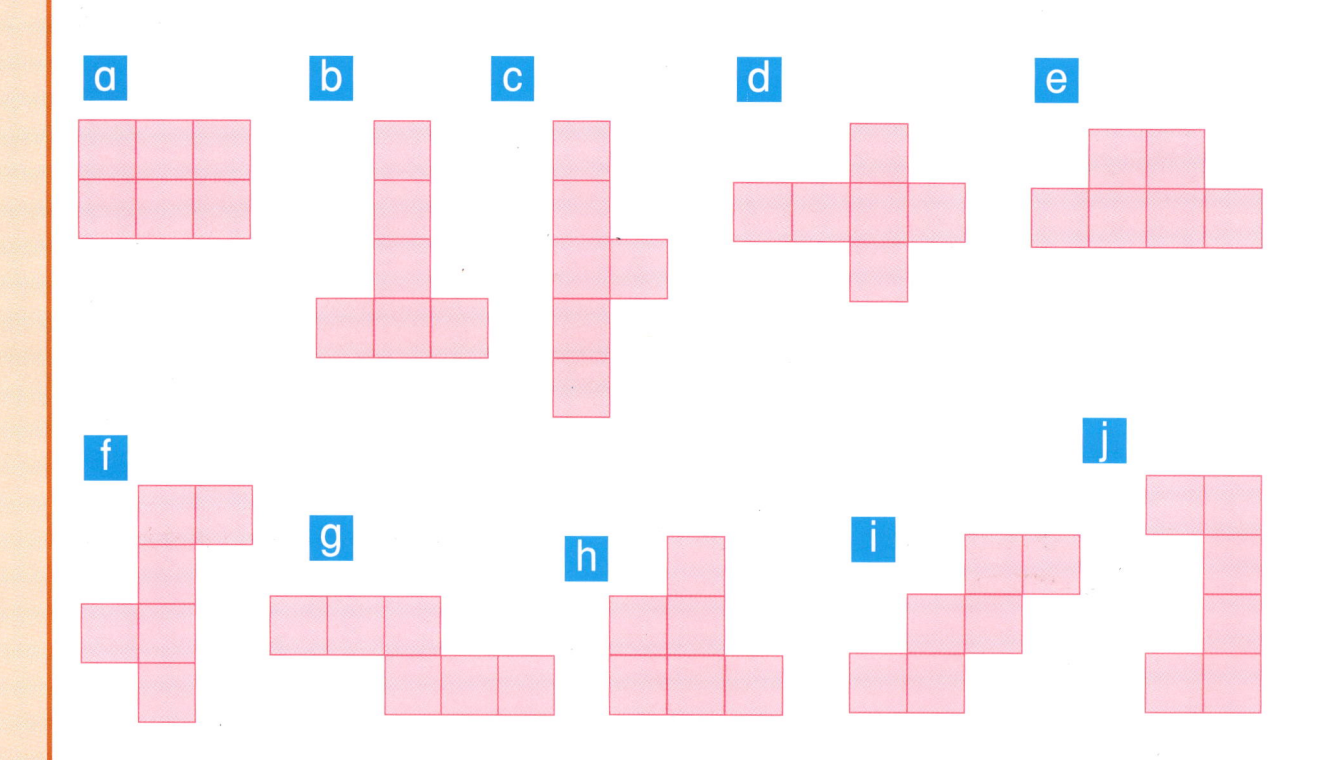

a   b   c   d   e

f   g   h   i   j

A3 You need squared paper, scissors and glue.

Choose a different hexomino which is the net of a cube. Draw it on squared paper and add tabs. Cut it out and fold it to make your cube. Glue it together using the tabs.

58   SS2 Properties of 3-D shapes

SS2.3 Visualising 3-D shapes

> **Key idea** Use clues to visualise parts of a 3-D shape you can't see.

Practical activity 1

You need interlocking cubes.

Work with a partner.

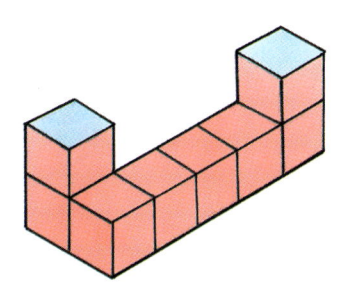

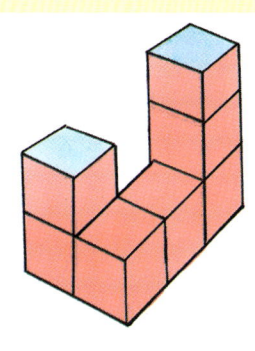

1
- **a** Use between 5 and 8 interlocking cubes to build a shape like the ones above.
- **b** Swap shapes with your partner. Predict the least number of cubes you will need to cover and join the ends of the shape. Check by building it.
- **c** Predict the least number of cubes you will need to turn the shape into a cuboid. Check by building it.
- **d** Repeat with different shapes.

Investigation A: Skeletal cubes

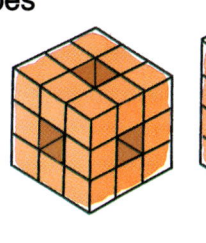

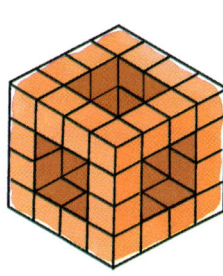

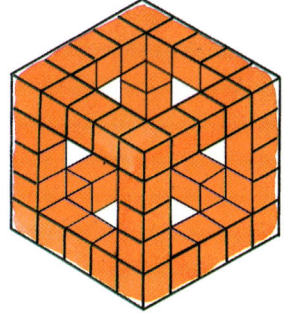

These drawings show skeletal cubes. They are built using cubes along the edges but leaving gaps in between.

1 How many cubes does it take to build
- **a** a $3 \times 3 \times 3$ skeletal cube?
- **b** a $4 \times 4 \times 4$ skeletal cube?
- **c** a $5 \times 5 \times 5$ skeletal cube?

2 Can you predict how many cubes you would need for a $6 \times 6 \times 6$ skeletal cube?

3 What pattern can you see in your answers?

SS2 Properties of 3-D shapes

1 **Investigation B: Visualising cubes**

Imagine you have 8 wooden cubes. You fit them together to make a 2 × 2 × 2 cube.

Then you paint the outside faces red.

How many cubes have:

3 red faces?

2 red faces?

1 red face?

0 red faces?

Record your results in a table like the one below.

size of cube	number of cubes with				total number of cubes
	3 red faces	2 red faces	1 red face	0 red faces	
2 × 2 × 2					
3 × 3 × 3					
4 × 4 × 4					
5 × 5 × 5					

2 What if... you build a 3 × 3 × 3 cube and, in the same way, paint the faces red?

How many cubes have 3 red faces? 2 red faces? 1 red face? 0 red faces?

Record the answers in the table.

3 Now trial a 4 × 4 × 4 cube.

Then trial a 5 × 5 × 5 cube.

Record your answers in the table each time.

4 Using the pattern, enter the results for a 6 × 6 × 6 cube.

Key idea	Use clues to visualise parts of a 3-D shape you can't see.

SS2 Properties of 3-D shapes

SS3.1 Reflections in 1 mirror line

> **Key idea** In a reflection matching vertices are the same distance from the mirror line.

★1 **Work with a partner.**

For each pair of shapes discuss whether it shows a reflection in a mirror line.

Answer yes or no.

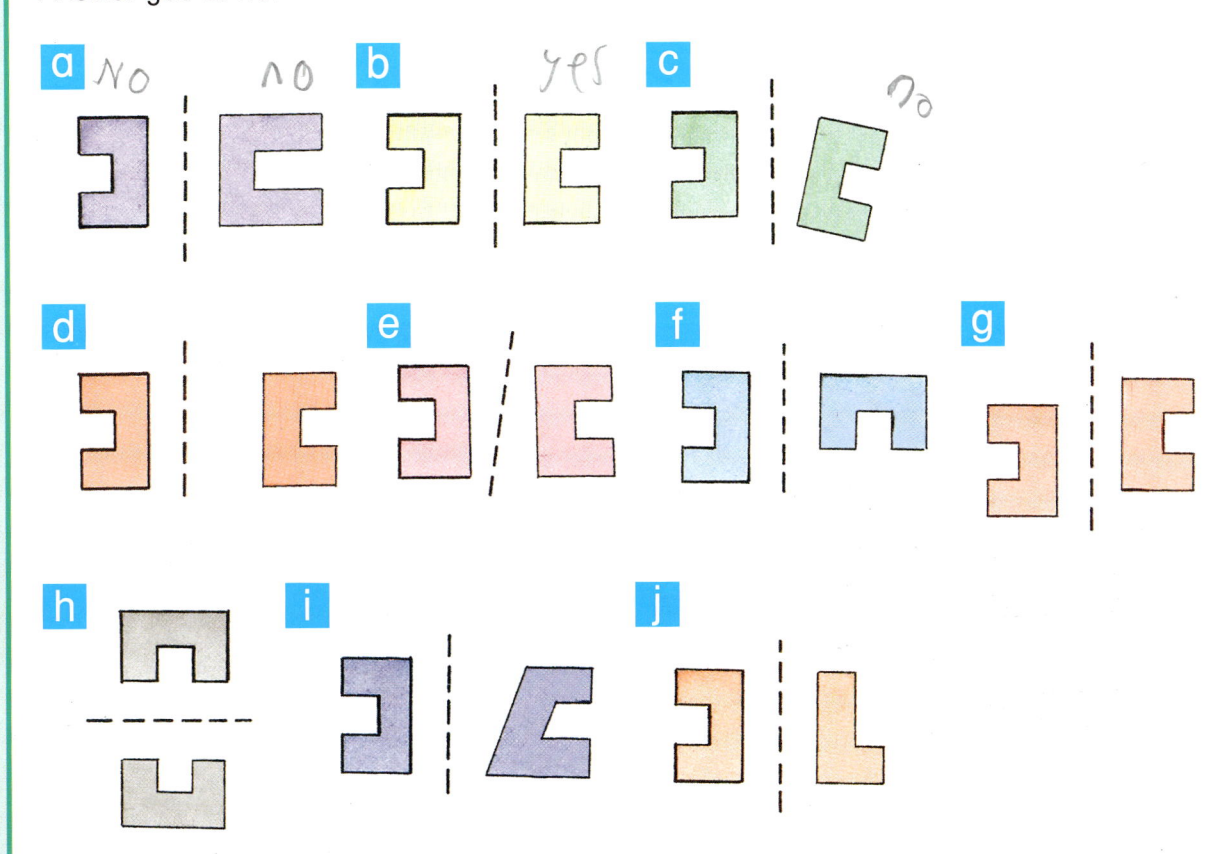

a. No   no
b. yes
c. no

d.
e.
f.
g.

h.
i.
j.

★2 **You need squared paper.**

Copy each shape and draw its reflection.

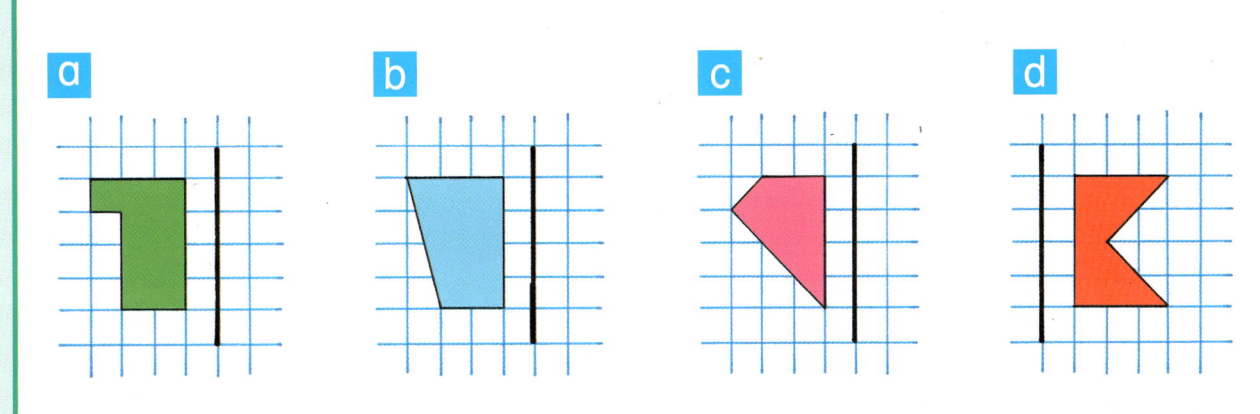

a.
b.
c.
d.

SS3 Reflective symmetry

SS3.2 Reflections in 2 mirror lines

Key idea	You can reflect a shape in 1 mirror line and then another.

A1 You need squared paper.

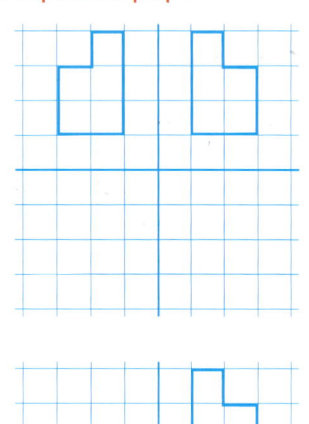

Copy this pattern and draw its reflection in the horizontal mirror line.

A2

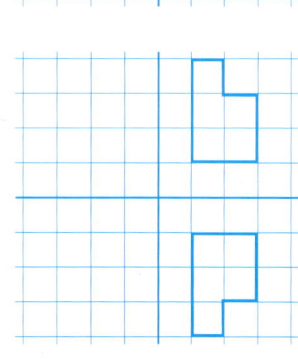

a Copy this pattern onto squared paper and draw its reflection in the vertical mirror line.

b What do you notice about your answers to A1 and A2a? Explain.

A3

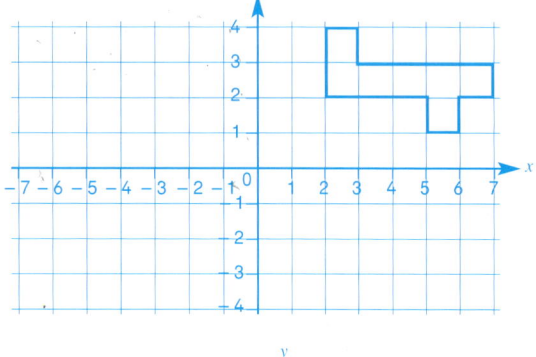

Copy this pattern onto squared paper and draw the reflection, first in the *y*-axis, then in the *x*-axis.

A4

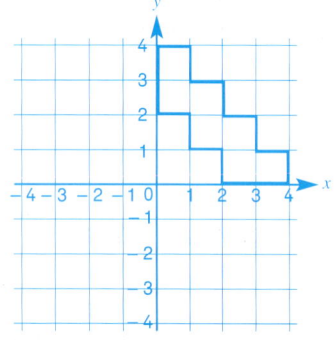

Copy this symmetrical pattern in the same way.

C1 Create your own pattern of lines parallel or perpendicular to the axes in the first quadrant. Draw the reflections in the *x*-axis and *y*-axis.

62   SS3 Reflective symmetry

SS3.3 Reasoning about symmetry

> **Key idea** You can make different shapes by reflecting pentominoes in different ways.

A1 You need squared paper.

You can make a new shape twice as large as a pentomino, by reflecting the pentomino in a mirror line along one edge.

For each pentomino below, find and draw 4 different ways to make the new shape.

a   b 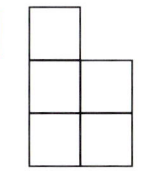   c

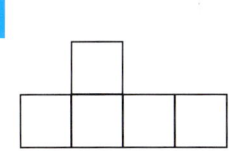

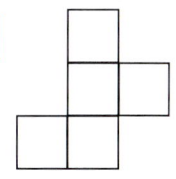

B1 You need squared paper.

How many different new shapes can you make by reflecting the pentominoes in a mirror line along one edge. Find and draw them.

a   b 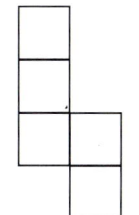   c 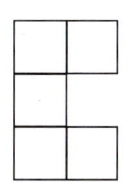   d

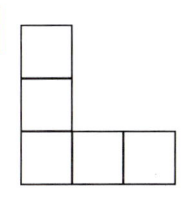

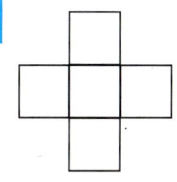

B2 Which of these other pentominoes only make 2 different new shapes?

a   b 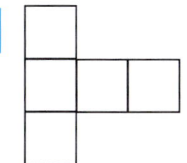   c

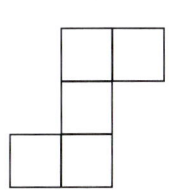

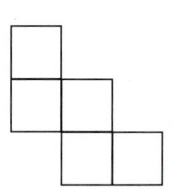

B3
a Which pentomino makes the least number of new shapes?

b Why do you think this is? Explain your ideas.

C1 Investigate how many new shapes you can make if you start with a hexomino and reflect it.

a Can you find hexominoes that make 4 different new shapes?

b How many hexominoes can you find that make 2 different new shapes?

c Can you find a hexomino that only makes 1 different new shape?

SS3 Reflective symmetry

63

SS4.1 Translations and 3-D shapes

| Key idea | You can sketch 3-D shapes by translating a 2-D shape and joining matching vertices. |

★1 You need squared paper.

a Copy this triangle.

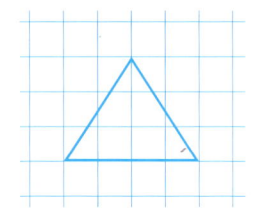

Translate it 5 squares to the right.

Now translate the second triangle 3 squares down.

Do the same for these shapes and translations.

b 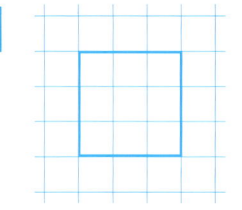
6 squares down
4 squares to the right

c 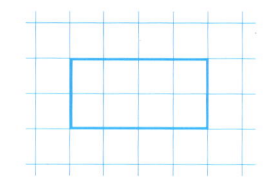
3 squares up
5 squares to the left

d 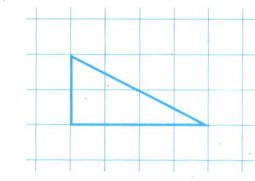
7 squares to the left
2 squares up

★2 You need a square, rectangle or triangle.

Draw round your shape carefully on squared paper.

Slide it to a new position and draw round it again.

Join matching vertices to make a skeleton drawing of a 3-D shape.

Name the 3-D shape you have drawn.

A1 You need squared paper.

Copy these shapes and translate each vertex by the amount shown. Join corresponding vertices and name the skeleton 3-D shape you have drawn.

a 1 right, 1 up

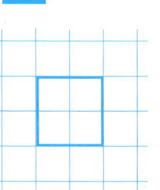

b 3 right, 4 down

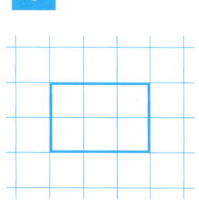

c 4 left, 5 up

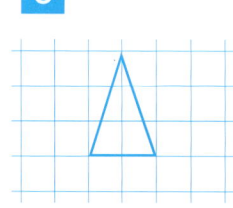

d 6 left, 4 down

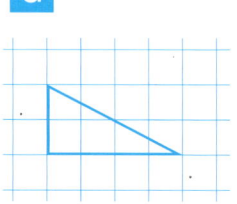

e 5 left, 2 down

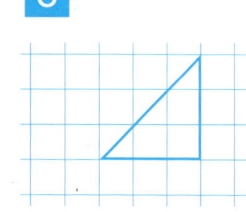

64   SS4 Translation

B1 You need squared paper.

Copy these shapes and translate vertices A, B, and C by the amount shown. Join corresponding vertices and draw any visible edges to make a solid 3-D shape. Shade or colour one of the faces.

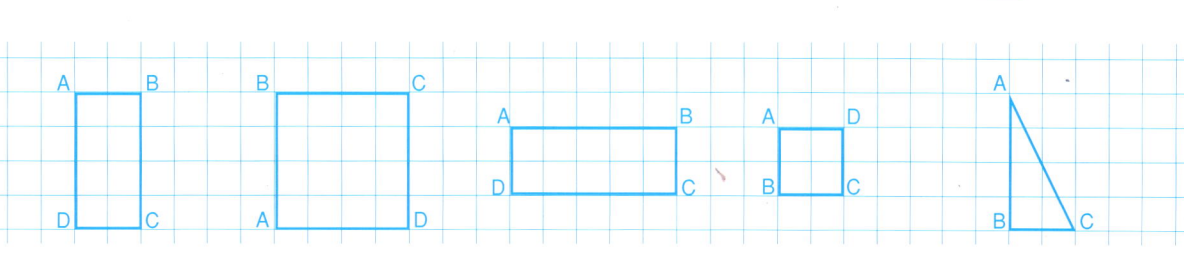

a	b	c	d	e
1 right, 1 up	2 left, 2 up	1 right, 4 up	6 left, 3 down	1 left, 2 down

C1 How many different ways can you draw solid prisms by translating this triangle?

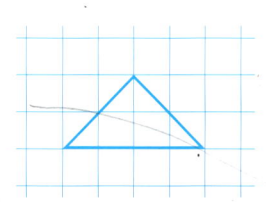

Explore what happens if you translate the triangle:

a. to the right only
b. to the left only
c. up only
d. down only
e. the same amount up as along
f. different amounts down and along

C2
a. How can you tell if 2 or 3 faces of the prism in C1 will be visible.
b. Is this true for other shaped triangles?
Discuss with a partner and test your ideas by drawing.

Key idea You can sketch 3-D shapes by translating a 2-D shape and joining matching vertices.

SS4 Translation

SS4.2 Translating patterns

> **Key idea** You can make repeating patterns by combining translations.

A1 You need squared paper.

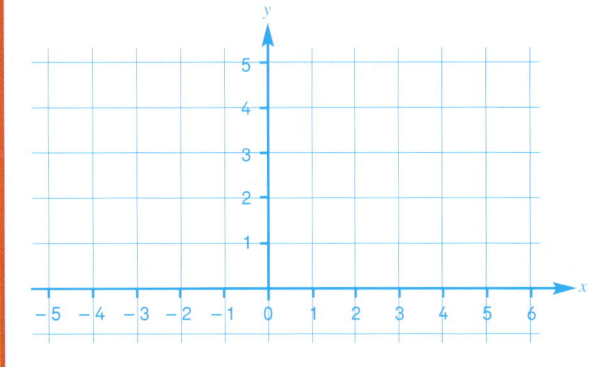

a Copy this set of axes on squared paper.

b Plot points (3, 4), (5, 4) and (5, 5).
Join them to make a triangle.

c Translate the triangle 6 squares to the left.

d Now translate the second triangle 3 squares down.

e Write the co-ordinates of the vertices of the third triangle you drew.

A2 Repeat A1 with points (1, 1), (3, 1) and (3, 2), and a translation of 2 squares up, followed by a translation of 5 squares to the left. Give the co-ordinates of the vertices of the third triangle.

A3 You need CM 41.

a Translate the triangle 5 squares left and draw its new position.

b Translate the second triangle 5 squares down, then 5 squares right and draw its new position.

c Keep repeating a and b to make a strip pattern.

A4 You need squared paper.

a Draw a rhombus in the top left hand corner of the sheet. Make a pattern by repeating the translation 4 right, 1 down.

b When you reach the edge of the paper, draw another shape on the left hand side of the page below the rhombus. Translate this shape in the same way as the original rhombus.

c Continue translating shapes until your pattern fills the page.

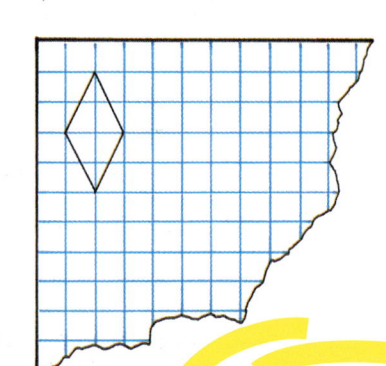

Make your shapes small so they don't overlap.

SS4 Translation

CM 41

B1 You need squared paper.

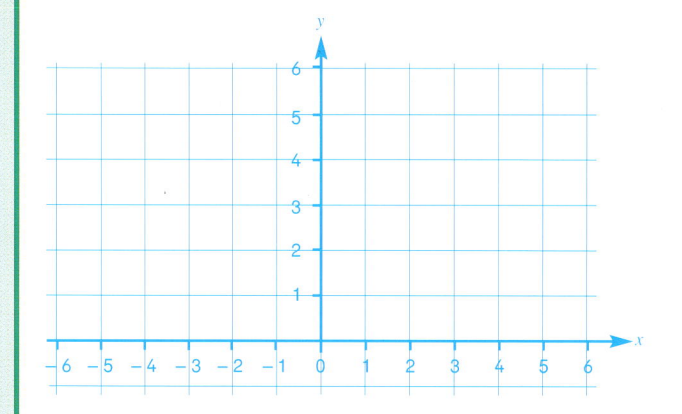

a Copy this set of axes. Plot and join points (3, 1), (5, 1), (6, 2) and (3, 3) to make a quadrilateral.

b Draw the quadrilateral after it has been translated 9 squares left, 1 square up.

c Translate this new quadrilateral 4 squares right, 2 squares up. Draw it and give the co-ordinates of each vertex.

B2

a Draw a new set of axes and plot points (−6, 2), (−5, 1), (−4, 2) and (−5, 3).

Draw the new quadrilateral after each of these translations:

b 2 right, 3 up **c** 7 right, 4 down **d** 5 left, 2 up

Start from the most recent shape each time.

e Give the co-ordinates of each vertex of the final quadrilateral.

B3 You need CM 41.

a Translate the triangle 2 down, 4 left. Draw its new position.

b Translate the second triangle 2 down, 4 right. Draw its new position.

c Keep repeating these new translations alternately to make a strip pattern.

B4 You need squared paper.

a Draw a kite in the bottom left hand corner. Make a pattern by repeating the translation 1 right, 7 up followed by the translation 2 right, 3 down.

b Find a way to complete the pattern so that it fills the whole page.

C1 Create a simple design for wrapping paper by combining translations of a shape or shapes.

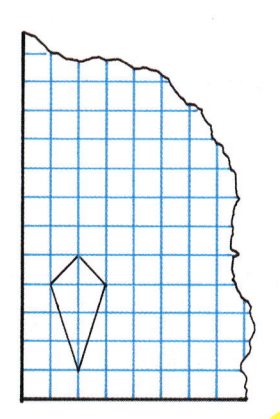

Choose translations which won't overlap.

| Key idea | You can make repeating patterns by combining translations. |

SS4 Translation

SS4.3 Translations in 4 quadrants

> **Key idea** You can find the distance and direction of a translation by looking at matching vertices.

A1 You need CM 42.

For each shape, do the first translation, then translate the shape again.

Give the co-ordinates of the final position.

a Shape A: first translation up 9, second translation left 8.

b Shape B: first translation right 8, second translation up 4.

c Shape C: first translation down 5, second translation right 5.

d Shape D: first translation left 7, second translation down 15.

A2 You need squared paper.

Draw axes and plot these shapes:

Shape J: (3, −2), (4, −2), (5, −4), (1, −4)

Shape K: (−3, −1), (−2, −1), (−1, −3), (−5, −3)

Shape L: (−4, 5), (−3, 5), (−2, 3), (−6, 3)

Shape M: (4, 4), (5, 4), (6, 2), (2, 2)

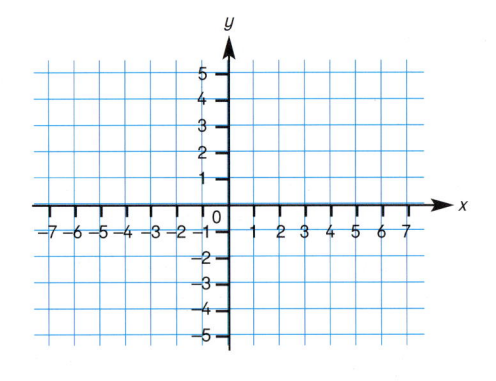

Identify the translation that moves:

a J to K **b** M to L **c** L to M **d** M to J **e** M to K

B1 You need squared paper.

Draw these axes.

a Draw shape A with vertices at (4, 2), (5, 1), (8, 3), (6, 4).
Plot the following translations, labelling the shapes B to G:

b right 2, down 3 **c** left 7, down 3

d left 6, down 1 **e** left 2, up 5

f right 1, up 5 **g** right 5, down 2

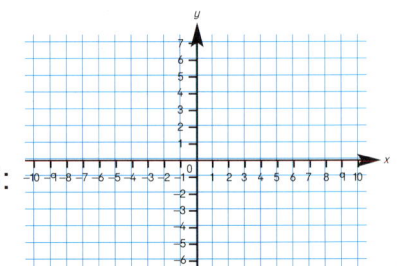

Start from the most recent shape each time

h What translation will move shape G back to position A?

B2 Draw axes on squared paper and plot these shapes:

Shape P: (6, 4), (6, 2), (8, 2), (8, 4), (7, 5)

Shape Q: (8, –1), (8, –3), (10, –3), (10, –1), (9, 0)

Shape R: (–4, –5), (–4, –7), (–2, –7), (–2, –5), (–3, –4)

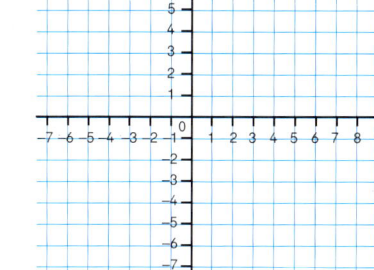

Shape S: (–7, 5), (–7, 3), (–5, 3), (–5, 5), (–6, 6)

Identify the translation that moves:

a Q to P **b** S to P **c** S to R

d R to Q **e** R to P **f** S to Q

C1 You need squared paper.

Work in a group of 3–6.

Play 'Tricky translations':

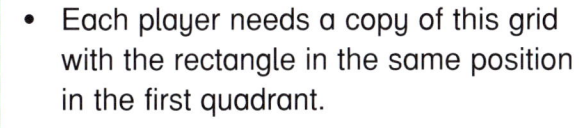

- Each player needs a copy of this grid with the rectangle in the same position in the first quadrant.

- One player chooses a translation that moves the rectangle to a new position in the grid and secretly draws its new position on their grid.

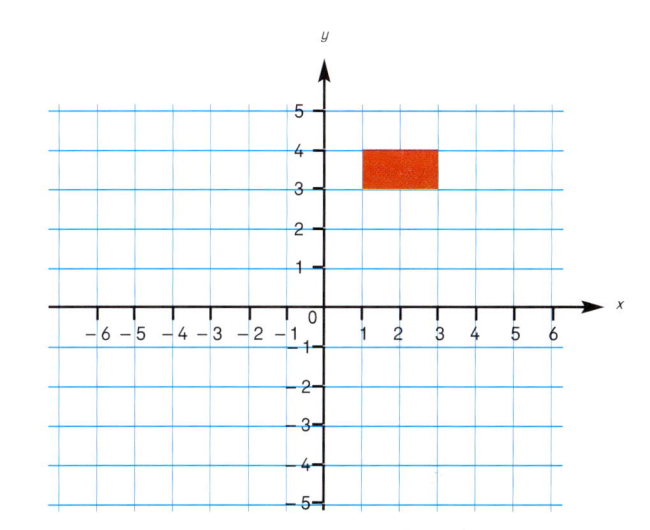

- They give one co-ordinate of the new position and the other players plot this point on their grids.

- The second player has a turn at guessing the translation.

- If they guess wrongly they are given another co-ordinate to plot and the next player has a turn at guessing.

- Continue until a player identifies the translation. All the players draw the new position of the rectangle.

- The player who guesses the answer chooses the next translation.

Key idea You can find the distance and direction of a translation by looking at matching vertices.

SS4 Translation

SS4.4 Translating and tessellating

Key idea	Some shapes can be translated to make a tessellating pattern.

This tessellating pattern is made by translating a hexomino.

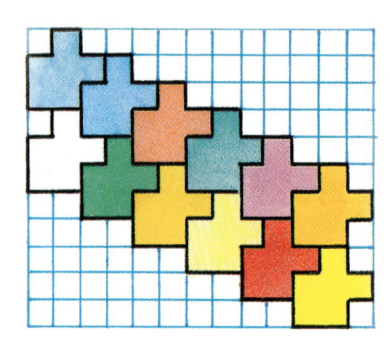

You need squared paper.

1. **a** Draw an L-shape in the middle of your squared paper.

    b Translate the L-shape right 1 and up 1 and draw the new position. Repeat several more times.

    c The opposite of right 1, up 1 is left 1, down 1. Use this translation to continue the pattern in the opposite direction.

    d Go back to the original L-shape. Use the translation right 1, down 3 to continue the pattern in another direction.

    e What is the opposite of right 1, down 3? Use this translation to extend the pattern further.

2. These are the 12 pentominoes:

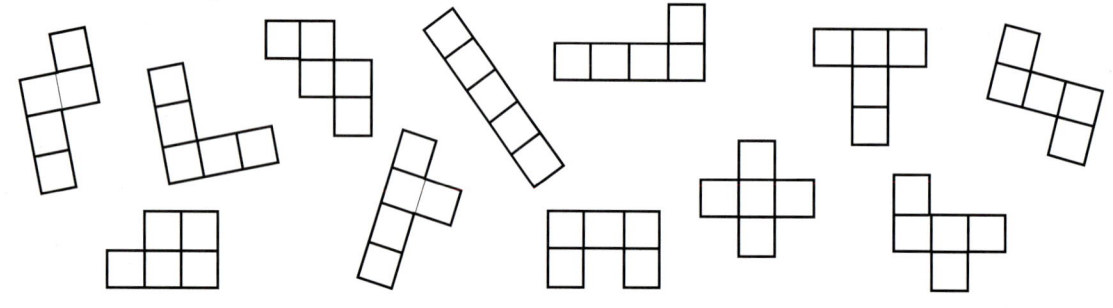

    Every pentomino tessellates. Most, but not all, of these tessellations can be made by repeated translations.

    Investigate this general statement. How many tessellations can you make using translation alone?

70   SS4 Translation

SS5.1 Intersecting lines

Key idea	Lines that cross each other are called intersecting lines.

★1   Draw a pair of intersecting lines.

★2   How many intersections?

a

b

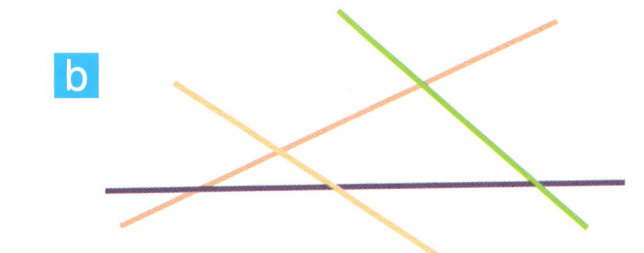

A1   Copy this diagram. Join each circle to every cross with a straight line.

How many intersections are there?

A2   The diagonals of a quadrilateral intersect once.

How many intersections can you find for the diagonals of a pentagon?

Check by drawing several different pentagons. Do you get the same answer every time?

A3   Do CM 43.

B1   This is a map of a rabbit warren. Each sleeping chamber must be linked to each entrance by a tunnel. The tunnels intersect at 3 points.

You can draw it as a diagram like this:

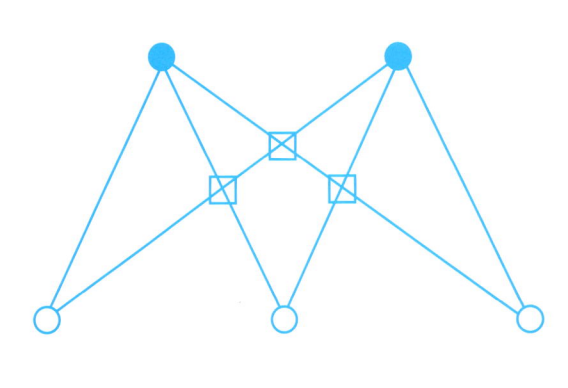

Copy this diagram and label it '3 sleeping chambers'.

SS5 Position and direction

B2 Draw a diagram to show how many intersections there will be if there are 2 entrances and 4 sleeping chambers.

B3 Draw another diagram to show the intersections for 2 entrances and 5 sleeping chambers.

B4 Look at your results so far. Can you see a pattern? Try to predict the number of intersections for 2 entrances and 6 sleeping chambers. Check by drawing.

B5 Explain any patterns you have found.

Use them to make predictions for up to 10 sleeping chambers.

C1 These 2 triangles overlap.

There are 2 intersections.

Can you draw an arrangement of 2 overlapping triangles that has

  a 4 intersections?

  b 6 intersections?

  c more than 6 intersections?

C2 Explain why it is not possible to draw 2 overlapping triangles with an odd number of intersections.

C3 Try 3 overlapping triangles.
Find an arrangement with the greatest possible number of intersections.

> **Key idea** Lines that cross each other are called intersecting lines.

SS5 Position and direction

SS5.2 Beyond the first quadrant

> **Key idea** When you extend the *x*-axis to the left beyond zero, you need to use negative numbers.

A1 You need CM 44.

This space map shows some of the planets in the Golden Dust Belt and some of the star stations at the edges of the Dust Belt.

Each has a landing site marked with a cross.

Give the co-ordinates for landing on

- **a** Firzon
- **b** Radgit
- **c** Pantor
- **d** Tircin
- **e** SS 01

A2 Mark these landing sites on the grid on CM 44.

- **a** Planet Zircon (–6, 7)
- **b** Planet Zarg (10, 9)
- **c** Planet Zeta (8, 6)
- **d** Planet Angam (0, 11)

A3 Draw star stations with landing sites at

- **a** (–2, 13) SS02
- **b** (0, 1) SS03
- **c** (4, 15) SS04

You need squared paper.

B1 Draw a pair of axes. Number the *x*-axis from –8 to 8 and the *y*-axis from 0 to 10.

- **a** Plot these points and join them in order:
  (–2, 10), (1, 9) (1, 7) (–2, 6) (–3, 8)

Complete the polygon and name it.

Repeat for the following sets of points.

- **b** (–6, 10) (–4, 9) (–6. 5) (–8, 6)
- **c** (2, 10) (5, 10) (6, 9) (6, 7) (3, 7) (2, 8)
- **d** (0, 5) (2, 4) (0, 3) (–3, 4)

B2 Use the same pair of axes.

- **a** (–4, 4), (–2, 2) and (–4, 0) are 3 of the vertices of a square. Plot them and find the co-ordinates of the 4th vertex.

- **b** 3 of the vertices of another square are given by the points (7, 3) (5, 0) and (2, 2). Find the co-ordinates of the 4th vertex.

SS5 Position and direction

SS5.3 Plotting co-ordinates in all 4 quadrants

> **Key idea**: When you extend the *x*-axis and the *y*-axis to include negative numbers, you can plot any point in a plane.

★1 Find the letters on the grid to crack the code.
(1, −4) / (3, 3) (0, −1) (1, −4) (−2, −4) (−3, 0) / (−1, 3) (−4, 3) / (1, −4) / (−4, −2)
(0, −1) (1, −4) (−1, −1) / (−4, 3) (0, 2) (4, −2) (−4, −2) (1, −4) (2, 1) (−3, 0)

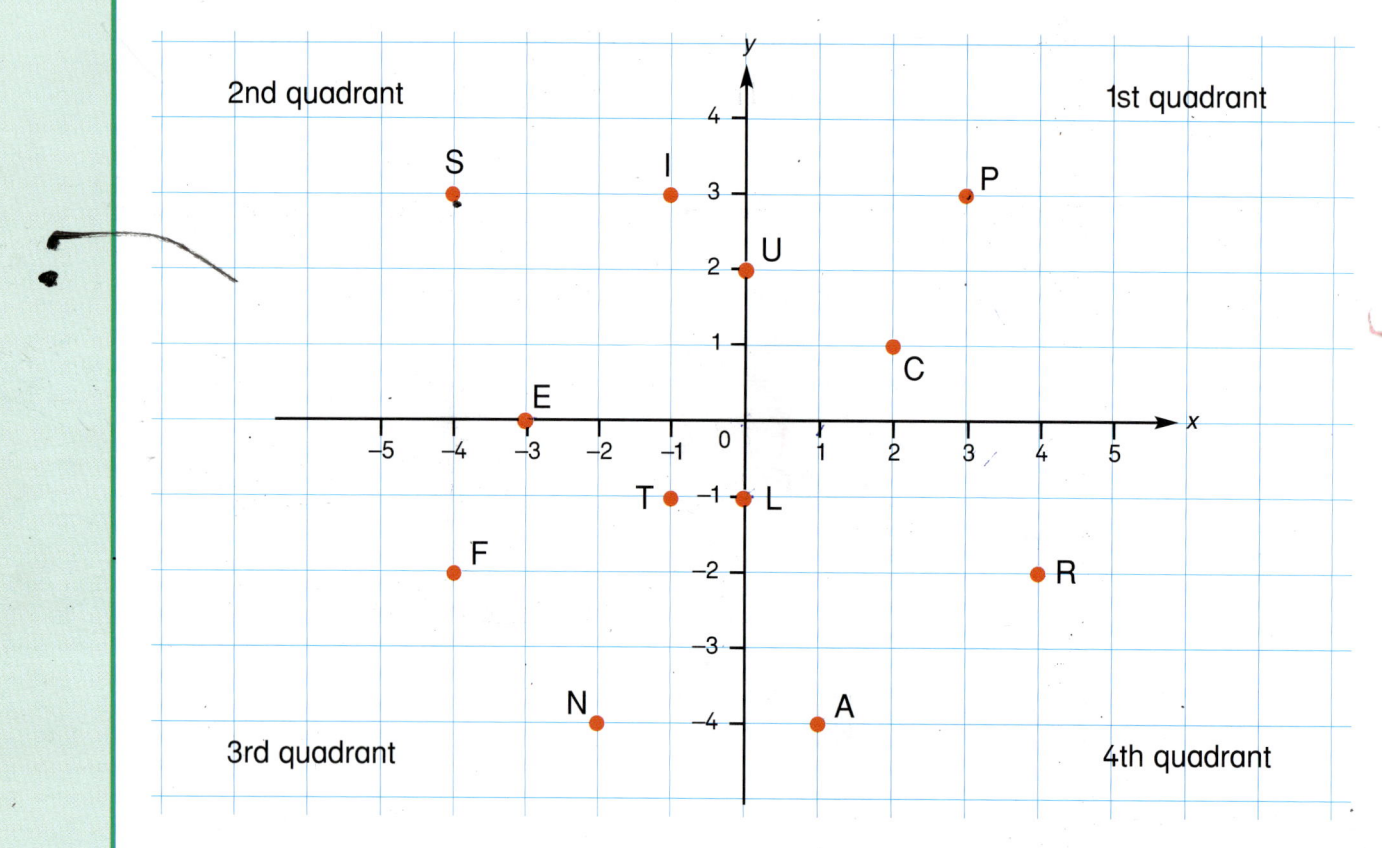

2nd quadrant · 1st quadrant
3rd quadrant · 4th quadrant

B1 You need squared paper.

a Draw a pair of axes. Number the *x*-axis from −9 to 9 and the *y*-axis from 0 to 12.

b
Pentagon	Reflection in *y*-axis
(3, 7)	
(6, 4)	
(8, 4)	
(8, 6)	
(5, 9)	

Copy this table.
Draw the pentagon and its reflection on your grid.
Complete the table.

74 SS5 Position and direction

c

Hexagon	Reflection in y-axis
(1, 2)	
(2, 0)	
(3, 1)	
(5, 2)	
(3, 3)	
(2, 4)	

Copy this table.
Draw the hexagon on your grid. Complete the table and check your answers by drawing the reflection on the grid.

d Draw a polygon of your own in the 1st quadrant and reflect it in the y-axis.

Draw a table and list the co-ordinates of your shape and its reflection.

C1

a Draw a pair of axes. Number the x-axis from −8 to 9 and the y-axis from −6 to 10.

b Plot and label the following points:

A (−3, 9)   B (1, 9)   C (5, 6)   D (7, 3)
E (8, −1)   F (6, −5)   G (0, −5)   H (−6, −5)
I (−8, −3)   J (−4, 1)   K (−3, 2)   L (−3, 5)
M (−6, 6)   N (0, 5)   O (1, 6)   P (3, 3)
Q (5, 0)   R (2, −1)   S (−2, −1)   T (0, 2)

c Join points to make an example of each of the following shapes:

- square
- rectangle
- rhombus
- parallelogram
- kite
- trapezium

Use every point at least once.

Key idea When you extend the x-axis and the y-axis to include negative numbers, you can plot any point in a plane.

SS5 Position and direction

SS5.4 Patterns in co-ordinates

> **Key idea** You can use what you know about reflection and co-ordinates to investigate patterns.

B1
You need CM 46.

a Plot the points A (3, 2), B(5, 4), C (5, 8), D (2, 5).

b Draw reflections of this shape in all 4 quadrants.

c Decide how to label the vertices of each reflection.

d Record the co-ordinates in a table.

e Discuss patterns in the co-ordinates with your teacher.

You need CM 46.

C1
a Plot the points P (−1, 5), Q (1, 8), R(4, 6).
Join them to make triangle PQR.

b Draw the reflection in the *y*-axis.
What do you notice about the co-ordinates of the reflection?

Reflect each vertex first.

c Reflect both triangles in the *x*-axis.

C2
a Draw a shape with vertices in both the 1st and the 4th quadrants.

b Investigate what happens to the co-ordinates when you reflect your shape in the *x*-axis.

SS6.1 Measuring angles

> **Key idea** An angle less than 90° is acute, an angle between 90° and 180° is obtuse, and angle of 180° is a straight line.

A1 Say whether each of these angles is acute, obtuse, a right angle or straight line.

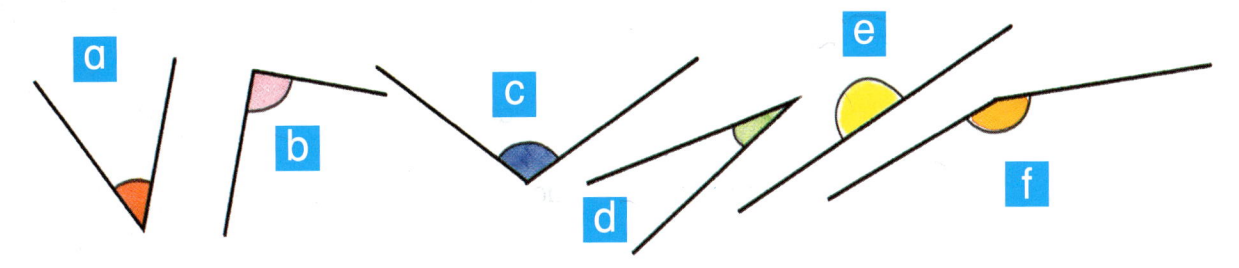

A2 Estimate the size of each of the angles in A1 in degrees.

A3 Do CM 47.

B1 What type of angles are these?

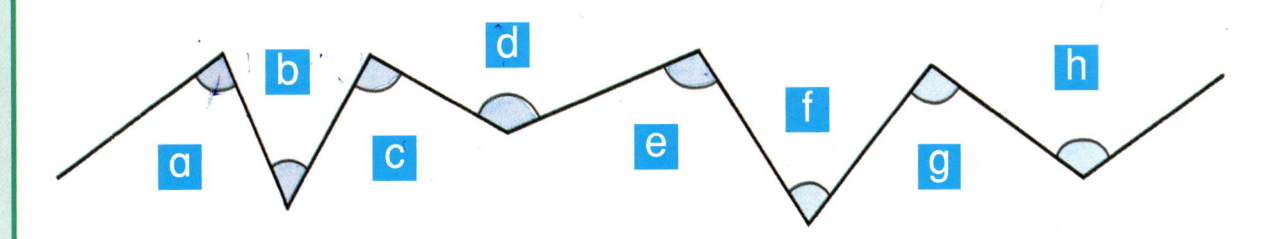

B2 Estimate each angle in B1.

B3 Do CM 48.

You need a protractor.

C1 Draw a hexagon with 1 acute and 5 obtuse angles.

Measure each angle.

C2 Draw a hexagon with 2 acute and 4 obtuse angles.

Measure each angle.

Make the drawings large enough to measure angles accurately.

C3 Can you draw a hexagon with 3 acute and 3 obtuse angles?

What about 4 acute and 2 obtuse angles?

Investigate.

SS6 Angle and rotation

SS6.4 Reflex angles

> **Key idea** A reflex angle is greater than 180° and less than 360°.

A1 Is each angle acute, obtuse or reflex?

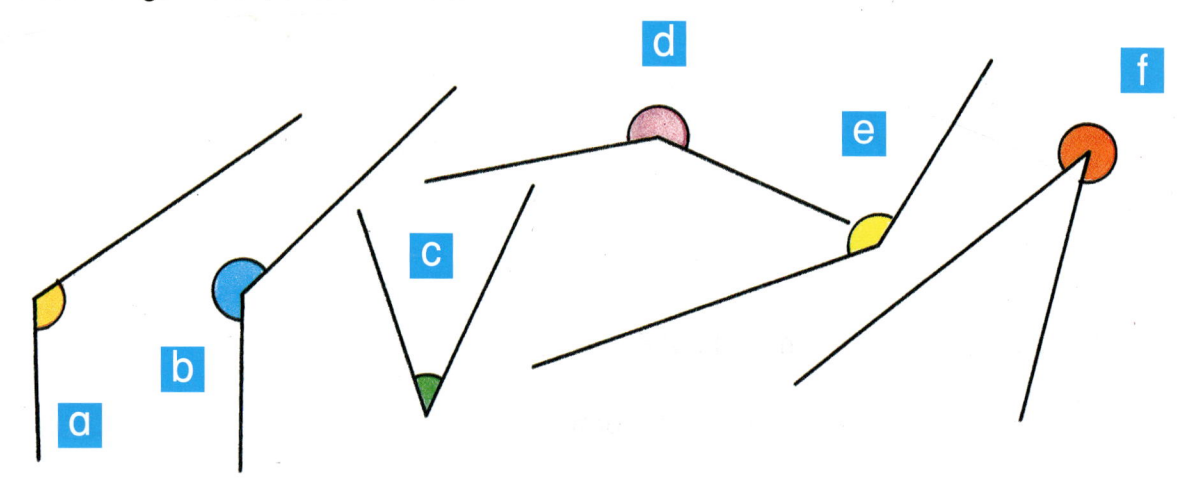

A2 Match these estimates and angles.

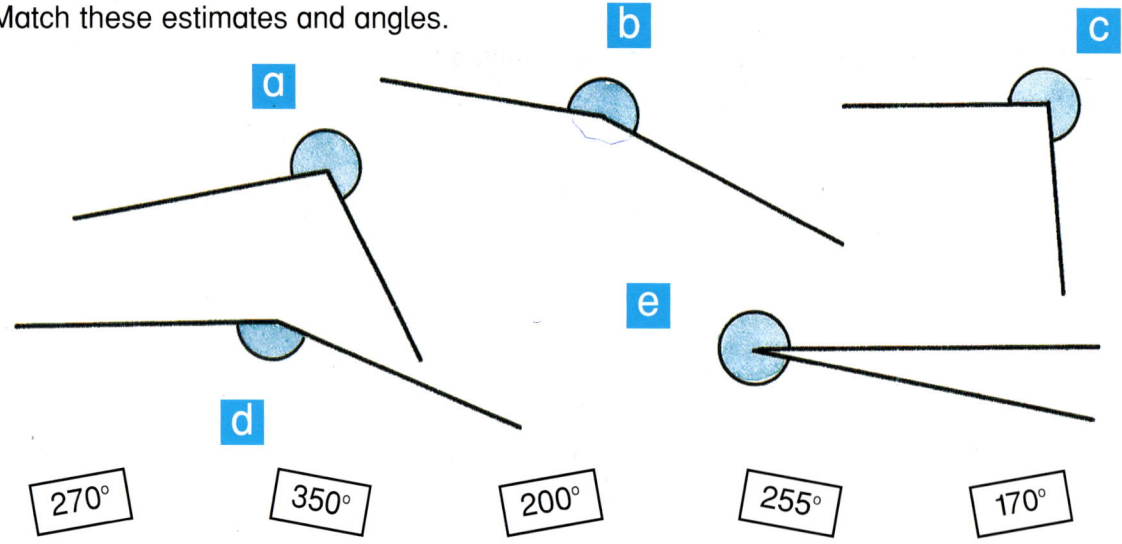

270°   350°   200°   255°   170°

A3 Calculate each angle marked with a letter.

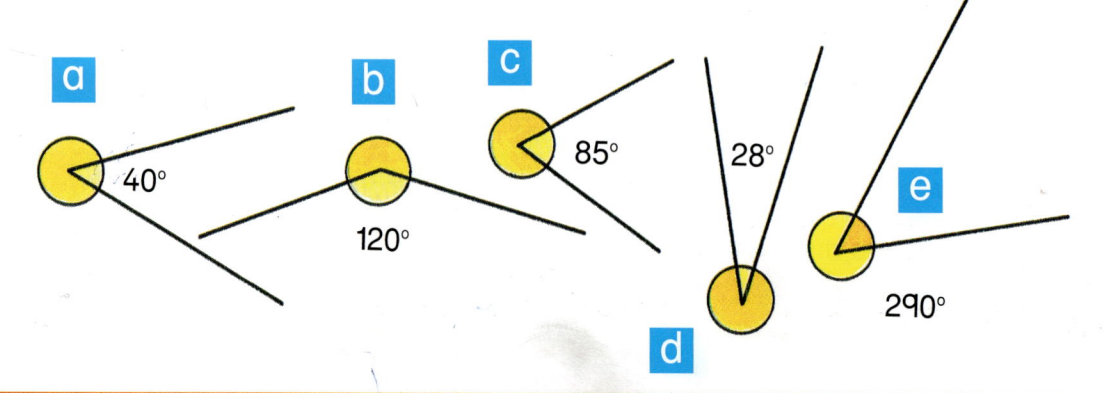

a 40°
b 120°
c 85°
d 28°
e 290°

78 SS6 Angle and rotation

B1 Do CM 50.

B2 Calculate the size of each angle marked with a letter.

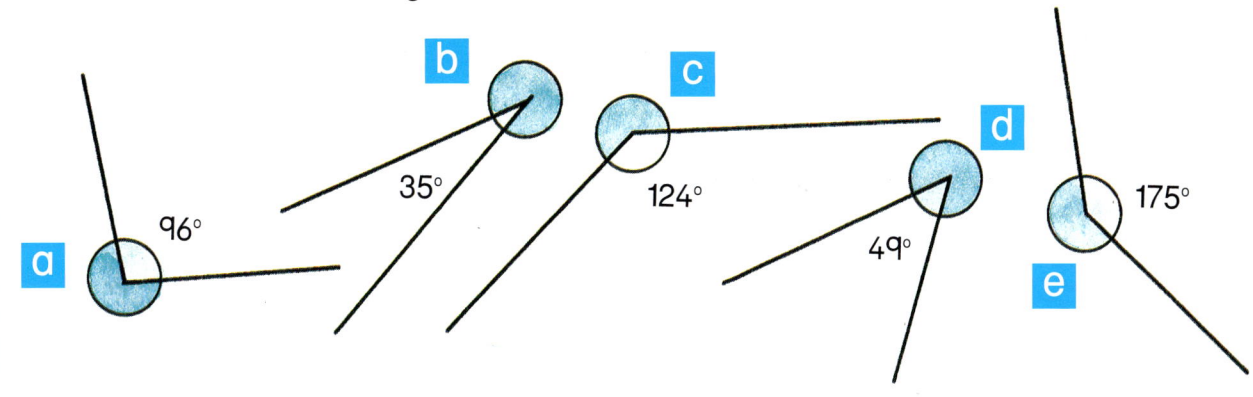

a 96°   b 35°   c 124°   d 49°   e 175°

You need a protractor.

C1 a Draw and label an angle of 83°.

　　　b Mark the reflex angle on your drawing.

　　　c Calculate its size.

C2 What size of acute angle must you draw if the reflex angle is 317°?

C3 Draw a reflex angle of 192°. Explain your method.

Key idea A reflex angle is greater than 180° and less than 360°.

SS6 Angle and rotation

HD1.2 Finding probabilities

> **Key idea** You can work out probabilities as fractions.

A1 Look at the spinners. For each one the outcomes are equally likely. Find the probabilities as fractions.

a) Probability of scoring 4 = $\frac{1}{\Box}$

b) Probability of scoring 2 = $\frac{\Box}{\Box}$

c) Probability of scoring 3 = $\frac{\Box}{\Box}$

A2 You need a partner.

Look at the pictures.

Talk about and record the possible outcomes when you:

a) throw the dice

b) choose a card

c) toss a coin twice

Does each event have equally likely outcomes?

A3 Find these probabilities for the events in A2:

a) probability of throwing a 5

b) probability of picking the 3 ♣

c) probability of getting 2 heads

A4 Look at this rectangular spinner.

List the possible outcomes.

Are they equally likely?

Explain your answer.

80 HD1 Probability

B1 You need CM 55 and crayons in red, blue, orange, yellow and green.

a Colour spinner 3 so that there is an equal chance of landing on red, blue, orange and yellow.

b Colour spinner 1 so that the probability of landing on red = the probability of landing on blue.

c Colour spinner 5 so that the probability of landing on orange = 1.

d Colour spinner 4 so that the probability of landing on orange = 0.

e Colour spinner 2 so that: the probability of landing on orange = $\frac{1}{6}$
the probability of landing on blue = $\frac{1}{3}$
the probability of landing on yellow = $\frac{1}{2}$.

f Colour spinner 6 so that: the probability of landing on red = 0
the probability of landing on blue = $\frac{2}{10}$
the probability of landing on yellow = $\frac{3}{5}$
the probability of landing on green = the probability of landing on orange.

B2 Look at these playing cards.

Hamish picks a card at random. Find the probability of his picking

a a number greater than 2

b a red card

c a heart card.

B3 Look at the spinners below.
- Which number(s) is the pointer most likely to stop on? Why?
- What is the probability of it stopping on an odd number?

a

b

C1 You need a pack of playing cards without the jokers.

If you pick one card at random, find the probability that it is

a   a King,

b   a diamond,

c   a black card,

d   a picture card (Jack, Queen or King).

C2 Use the cards to investigate more probabilities.

Key idea You can work out probabilities as fractions.

D1.3 Using a 0–1 scale for probabilities

> **Key idea** All probabilities lie on a scale from 0 (impossible) to 1 (certain).

B1 Courtney bought 6 packets of salad seeds.

He took out all the sachets of seeds and got them mixed up by mistake.

He sows a packet and wonders what will come up.

What is the probability that it will be

a lettuce? **b** parsley or coriander? **c** not spring onions?

Show the probabilities on a 0–1 scale.

B2 Natalia tossed 2 coins.

a List the possible outcomes.

b Put the probabilities for these outcomes on a 0–1 scale:

no heads   1 head   at least 1 head

B3 Design a spinner for a game so that the probability of scoring 1, 2, 3, 4, 5 or 6 is like this:

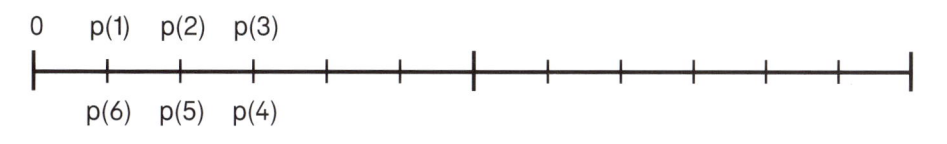

```
0   p(1) p(2) p(3)
|----+----+----+----+----+----+----+----+----+----+
     p(6) p(5) p(4)
```

p(1) means the probability of scoring 1

Use a protractor to divide a circle into 12 equal sections.

HD1 Probability

83

C1 Investigate these problems.

You need 3 different pairs of gloves.

Mrs Potts has twins called Alice and Tom.

Alice's gloves are yellow and Tom's are green but today they were all in such a rush that this is what happened:

She pulled out 1 glove and then another without looking and put them both on Tom.

Start by listing all possible outcomes.

a What is the probability that she ended up with a pair that fitted him (one right-handed and one left-handed)?

b What is the probability of pulling out a matching pair of gloves?

c What is the probability of pulling out Tom's green pair?

C2 Mrs Matthews has triplets called Ben, Katy and Toby.

She has 3 pairs of gloves in her bag.

Investigate the probability that the first two gloves she pulls out are a matching pair.

What if they are a matching pair and she pulls out another two gloves? What is the probability that these are a matching pair?

What if...?

Continue the investigation with your own questions and record your findings.

Key idea | All probabilities lie on a scale from 0 (impossible) to 1 (certain).

D1.4 Experimenting to find probabilities

> The more times you repeat an experiment, the closer you get to the probability you expect.

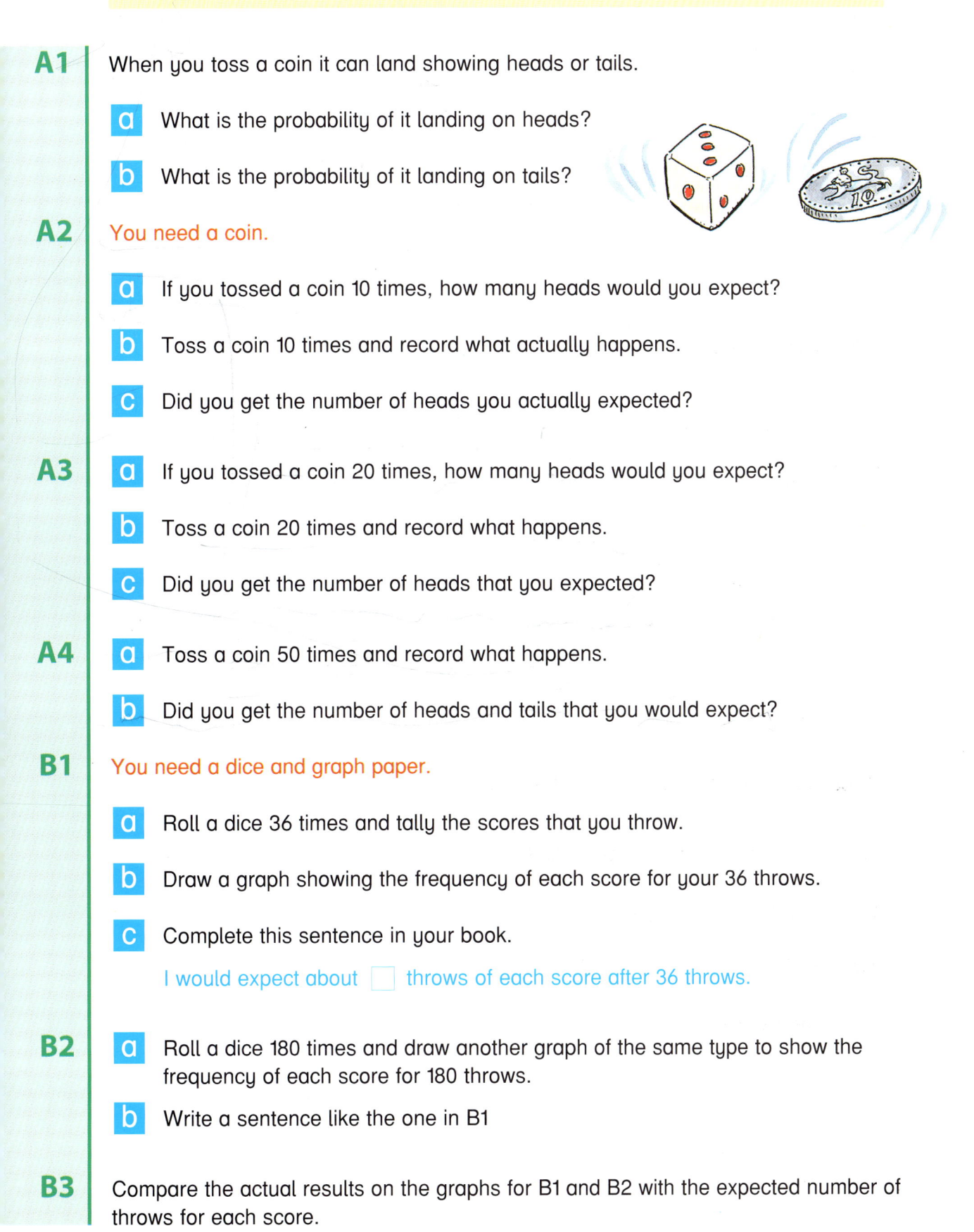

A1 When you toss a coin it can land showing heads or tails.

a What is the probability of it landing on heads?

b What is the probability of it landing on tails?

A2 You need a coin.

a If you tossed a coin 10 times, how many heads would you expect?

b Toss a coin 10 times and record what actually happens.

c Did you get the number of heads you actually expected?

A3 **a** If you tossed a coin 20 times, how many heads would you expect?

b Toss a coin 20 times and record what happens.

c Did you get the number of heads that you expected?

A4 **a** Toss a coin 50 times and record what happens.

b Did you get the number of heads and tails that you would expect?

B1 You need a dice and graph paper.

a Roll a dice 36 times and tally the scores that you throw.

b Draw a graph showing the frequency of each score for your 36 throws.

c Complete this sentence in your book.

I would expect about ☐ throws of each score after 36 throws.

B2 **a** Roll a dice 180 times and draw another graph of the same type to show the frequency of each score for 180 throws.

b Write a sentence like the one in B1

B3 Compare the actual results on the graphs for B1 and B2 with the expected number of throws for each score.

C1 You need a set of dominoes.

Look at the dominoes.

Each half can have 0, 1, 2, 3, 4, 5 or 6 dots.

a Write down the total number of dots on each domino.

b There are 28 dominoes in a complete set. Write a list of all possible totals.

C2 5 children took turns to mix up a set of dominoes and pick one randomly. They recorded the total number of dots each time and put the domino back. Here is a graph of their results.

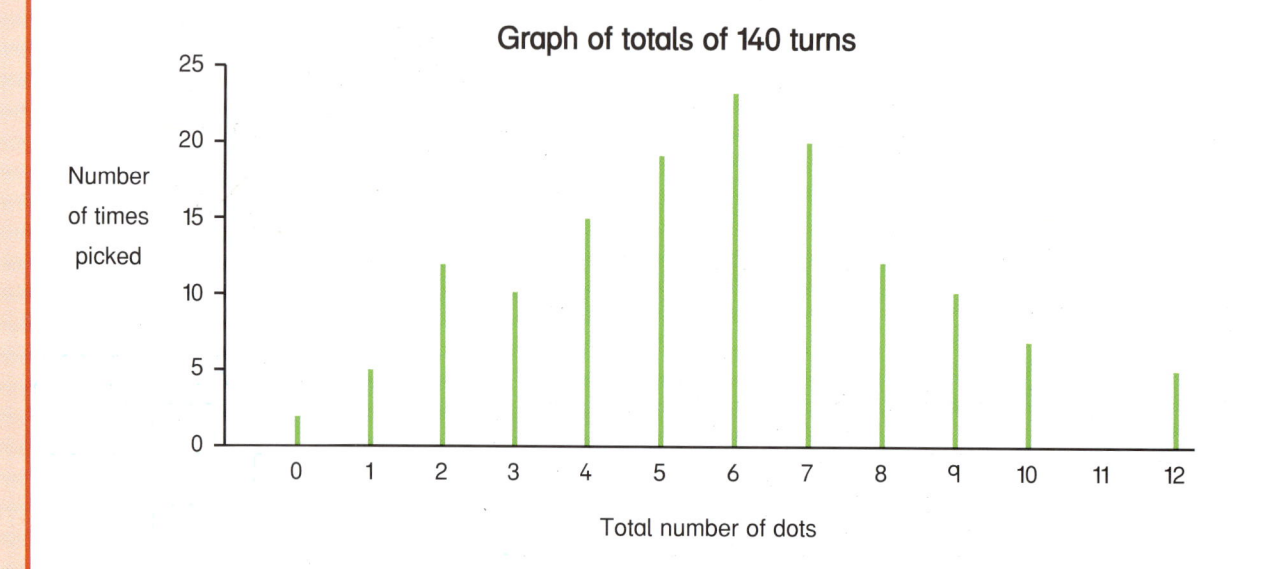

Graph of totals of 140 turns

Number of times picked vs Total number of dots

a Which totals are picked the number of times you would expect? Explain your reasoning.

b Explain why it is not surprising that a total of 11 was not picked at all.

| Key idea | The more times you repeat an experiment, the closer you get to the probability you expect. |

86 HD1 Probability

D2.2 Mean, median, mode and range 1

> **Key idea**
> The mean of a set of numbers is the sum of the numbers divided by the number in the set.
> The median is the middle number once the numbers have been arranged in order of size.
> The mode of a set of numbers is the number which occurs most frequently.

A1 Copy the blue columns from the frequency chart below. Total the number of each colour in all the bowls of sweets.

Colour	Bowl 1	Bowl 2	Bowl 3	Bowl 4	Total	Mean	Median	Mode	Range
Red	4	5	6	5					
Orange	3	4	7	6					
Green	5	7	4	4					
Brown	4	3	6	7					
Yellow	7	7	3	3					
Pink	6	6	5	3					

A2 Divide the total by the number of bowls to find the mean for each colour and add this information to the chart.

A3 What is the median number for each colour? Show your working for this in your book.

A4 Find the mode (if there is one) and range for each colour, and complete the table.

HD2 Organising and interpreting data 1

Children were divided into 6 teams for the school's sports day. There were four events and different numbers of children took part in each event.

Event	Team members' scores		
Netball shoot	Mars 4, 6, 3, 8, 4	Jupiter 7, 10, 3, 8, 7	Pluto 1, 5, 6, 4, 9
	Saturn 2, 7, 9, 4, 8	Mercury 7, 4, 1, 2, 6	Venus 3, 8, 6, 7, 6
Bean bags in a bucket	Mars 4, 2, 6, 3, 1, 4	Jupiter 7, 3, 7, 9, 6, 4	Pluto 2, 4, 3, 5, 4, 6
	Saturn 5, 2, 5, 4, 8, 6	Mercury 2, 6, 5, 3, 8, 6	Venus 4, 10, 9, 3, 6, 6
Bat and ball	Mars 10, 12, 8, 10	Jupiter 7, 7, 8, 6	Pluto 2, 4, 3, 5, 4, 6
	Saturn 9, 9, 8, 6	Mercury 10, 9, 11, 10	Venus 6, 6, 9, 11
Football shoot	Mars 4, 3, 8, 2, 3, 5, 3	Jupiter 10, 8, 7, 3, 4, 5, 5	Pluto 7, 3, 10, 8, 9, 3
	Saturn 5, 9, 8, 6, 3, 2, 2	Mercury 4, 9, 7, 7, 5, 2, 1	Venus 9, 8, 8, 5, 6, 4

B1 Which team has the highest mean score for bat and ball?

B2 Which team's median score for the football shoot is **a** highest? **b** lowest?

B3 **a** What is the mean team score for the netball shoot?

b How many teams' scores were higher than the mean team score?

B4 **a** What is the overall median score for the bean bag activity?

b Were any individual teams' median scores higher than this?

c What is the overall mode for this activity?

B5 Can you find a way to decide which is the most successful team overall? Explain how.

You need a metre stick and a calculator. Work with your group.

C1 Measure the height of everyone in your group. Use a calculator to find the mean height.

C2 What is the median height of your group?

C3 How do you think the mean and median heights would change if you measured your whole school? Give reasons for your answer.

D2.3 Pie charts 1

> **Key idea** | Pie charts represent data in a way that shows proportions.

A1 You need a copy of CM 59.

This pie chart shows the type of sports preferred by 8 children.

Sports children like

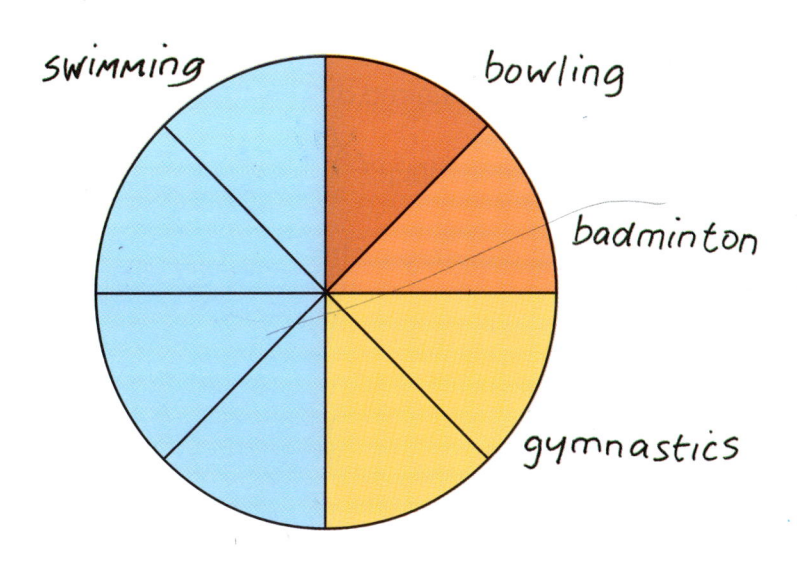

(Pie chart divided into 8 equal sections showing: swimming, bowling, badminton, gymnastics)

Find out how many children preferred each sport. Complete the chart on CM 59 Using the data from the pie chart. Remember to add a title to the first column.

A2 Ask 8 children what their favourite sport is. Give them a list to choose from. Use the pie chart on CM 59 to show your results.

Remember to give your chart a title and to label each section.

A3 On the back of the sheet write down the most and least popular sports from A2.

HD2 Organising and interpreting data 1

B1 You need CM 59.

Work with your teacher to find out some children's favourite flavours of crisp. Use this information to complete the frequency chart. Remember to add a title to the first column.

B2 Find out what fraction of the total group like plain crisps best.
Repeat for all the other flavours.

B3 Complete the pie chart to show your results.

C1 Class 6H did a survey of favourite subjects among their class of 32.
Use the pie chart to answer these questions.

a Which subject was the most popular? *information technology*

b What fraction of the children preferred art?

c Which subjects were equally popular?

d What fraction of the class preferred maths?

e How many children preferred history?

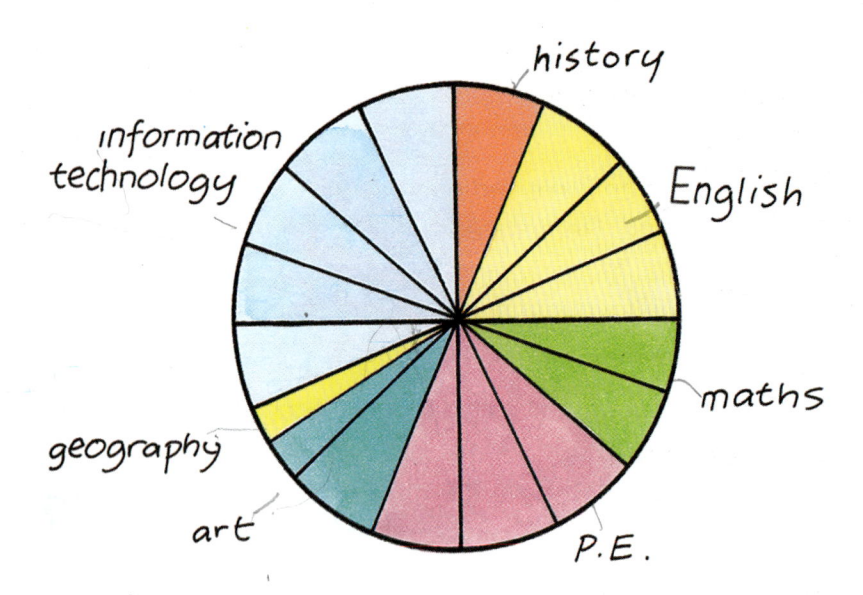

Key idea Pie charts represent data in a way that shows proportions.

D2.4 Line graphs 1

| Key idea | A line graph can show a trend in a set of data and can be used to find intermediate values. |

A1 You need squared paper.

Class 6W have been investigating which sleeping bag filling would keep you the warmest. They measured the temperature of the water every 5 minutes.

Here are the results.

Time (minutes)	Temperature in °C		
	No filling	Feather filling	Man-made filling
0	60°	60°	60°
5	32°	57°	46°
10	29°	53°	40°
15	28°	48°	36°
20	25°	42°	29°
25	22°	36°	25°

Use a piece of squared paper to draw a line graph to show 6W's results. Show all the fillings on the same set of axes. You could draw each line in a different colour and make a key to identify each line.

A2 What can 6W find out from their investigation?

B1 Children have used a computer program connected to a thermometer to measure the temperature of their classroom for 12 hours. This is the graph the computer created.

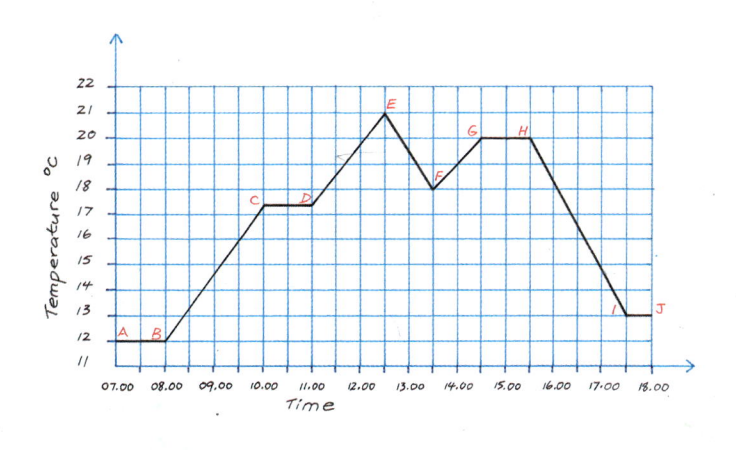

What is the temperature at

- **a** 08:00?
- **b** 10:00?
- **c** 13:00?
- **d** 16:00?

B2 At what times is the temperature

- **a** 12°C?
- **b** 21°C?
- **c** 19°C?
- **d** 17°C?

B3 Explain what is happening to the temperature between these points.

A→B   B→C   C→D   D→E   E→F   F→G   G→H   H→I   I→J

C1 Give some possible reasons for the shape of the graph.

HD2 Organising and interpreting data 1

HD3.1 Testing a hypothesis 2

| Key idea | You can organise data to test a hypothesis. |

★1 Here are the scores for 2 spelling tests.

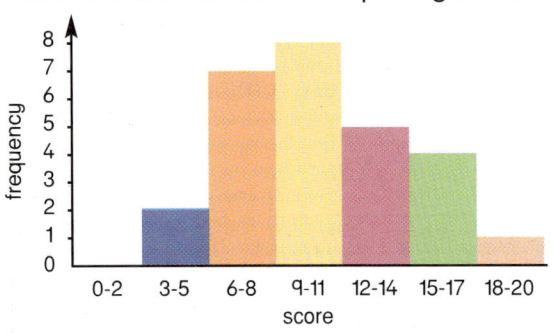

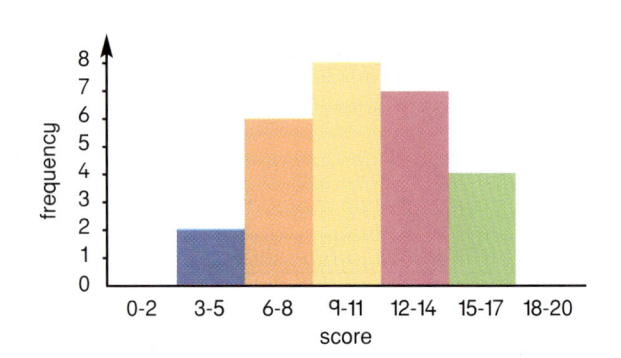

Look at the chart for week 1.

Are these statements true or false?

a Nobody scored more than 17 points.

b The most common scores were between 6 and 8.

c 3 children had full marks.

d Most people scored more than 8 out of 20.

A1 Look at the chart for week 1.

Are these statements true or false, or can't you say?

a Nobody scored less than 4 points.

b More children scored over 11 than scored less than 9.

A2 How many children took the test in week 1?

A3 The teacher expected that most of the class would score more than 11 points.

Did this happen in week 1?

B1 Look at the results for week 2.

Do you think that the test was easier or harder than in week 1. Explain your reasons.

C1 Make up some true/false/maybe statements of your own for the data from week 2.

Explain why you think they are true or false or why you are unable to tell.

92 HD3 Organising and interpreting data 2

D3.2 Mean, median, mode and range 2

The mean, median and mode give useful information about a set of data.

A1 You need a calculator.

These are the scores out of 20 for 15 children who had a test on the 7, 8 and 9 times tables:

10 17 12 19 12 15 18 14 17 14 12 19 20 14 12

- **a** Use a calculator to add up the scores and find their total.
- **b** Divide the total by the number of scores, 15, to find the mean. What is it?
- **c** Write the scores in order, starting with the smallest.
  What is the median (the middle value)?
- **d** Which score was the most common (the mode)?

A2
- **a** Look at your mean, median and mode for A1.
  Which do you think would be the most useful to the teacher? Why?
- **b** Which of the three values do you think would be the least useful to the teacher? Why?

B1

Here are some prices for houses in Bishop's Ford and in Great Camlow.

What is the mean price in each area? Use a calculator to help you.

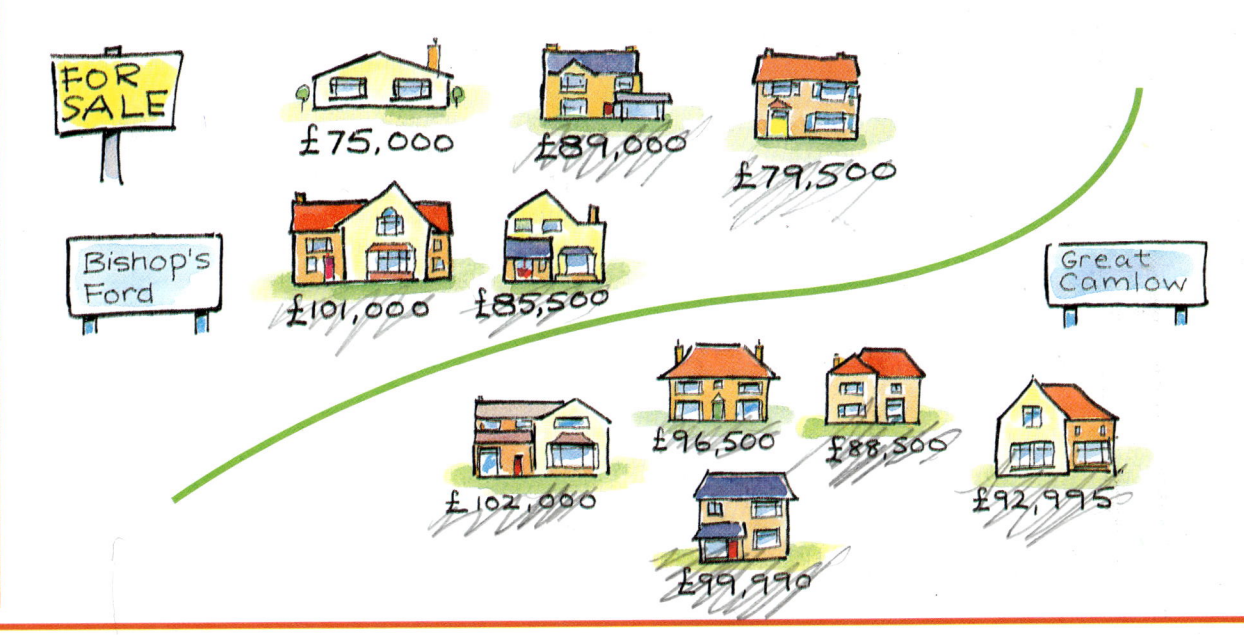

Bishop's Ford:
£75,000   £89,000   £79,500   £101,000   £85,500

Great Camlow:
£96,500   £88,500   £92,995   £102,000   £99,990

HD3 Organising and interpreting data 2

B2 A clothing company makes caps.

In a survey it collected this data about head sizes.

Circumference of head (cm)
44
44
46
44
47
55
49
46
48

a Find the mean, the median and the mode of these sizes.

b Which would you recommend the company uses as the size to make most of their caps? Why?

C1 This label has been ripped so we are unsure whether it is the mean, the median or the mode that is 24.

a Make up some data for 5 packets of these seeds that have a mean of 24.

b Repeat **a** for the median and the mode.

C2 Do the same as you did in C1 for this brand of seeds, where either the mean, the median or the mode is 28.

C3 If both packets of seeds cost 50p, it would seem that Plantum seeds are better value than Growlots.

Can you make up some data as you did in C1 and C2 that shows that you might be better off buying Growlots?

You do not have to use the same type of value for each brand.

Key idea | The mean, median and mode give useful information about a set of data.

D3.3 Pie charts 2

> **Key idea** | Pie charts present data in a way that shows fractions and percentages.

The school cook is choosing the menu for next week. She carried out a survey of children's favourite foods to help her decide. She asked 10 children. Here are the results.

Main course pie chart: Chicken nuggets, hot dogs, baked potatoes, spaghetti bolognaise

Pudding pie chart: chocolate sponge, fruit, jam doughnut, ice cream

The cook needs some help to interpret the results from the pie charts.

★1 What are the most popular choices?
   a main course   b pudding

★2 What are the least popular choices
   a main course   b pudding

★3 How many children voted for each food? Find out by counting the divisions for each food.
   a spaghetti bolognaise   b baked potato   c chicken nuggets
   d jam doughnuts   e chocolate sponge   f fruit

A1 Look at the pie chart and decide what fraction of the children preferred
   a hot dogs   b spaghetti bolognaise   c chicken nuggets
   d baked potato   e ice cream   f jam doughnuts
   g fruit   h chocolate sponge

C1 Carry out a survey of the whole class to find their favourite main courses and puddings from the choices given above. Present your data in a frequency chart. Why would it be easier to use a computer to present this data as a pie chart?

HD3 Organising and interpreting data 2

95

HD3.4 Line graphs 2

> **Key idea** Line graphs can be used to find intermediate values.

★1

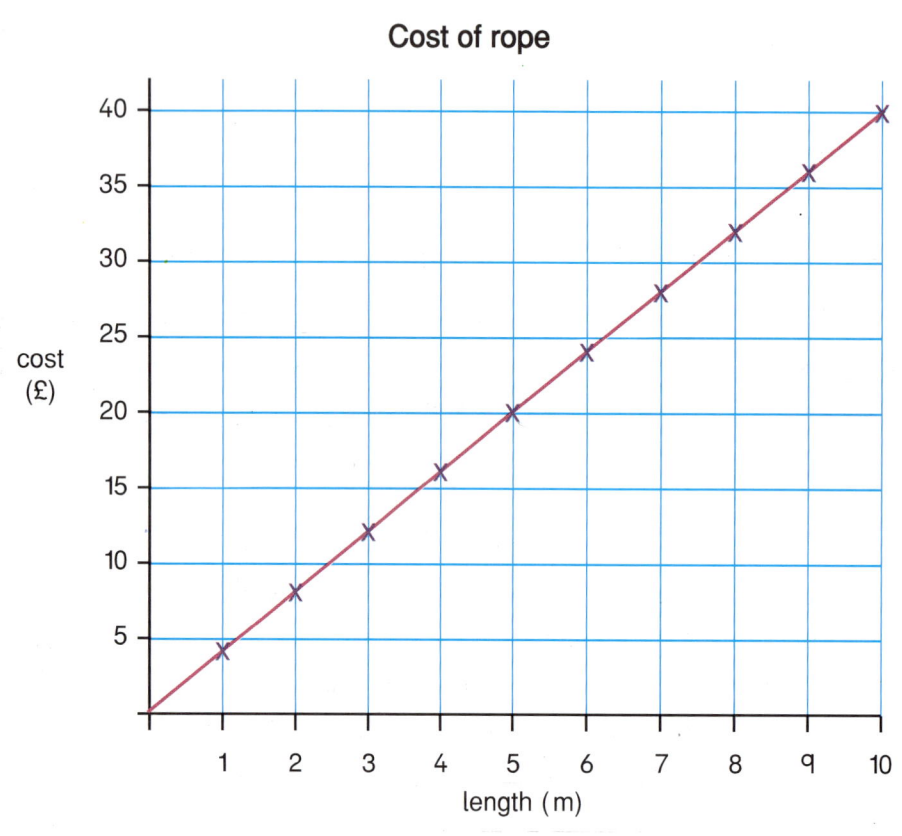

Cost of rope

(graph showing cost (£) vs length (m), linear from origin through (1,4), (2,8)... to (10,40))

Use the graph to find out the cost of:

a 5 metres　　**b** 7.5 metres　　**c** 3 metres

★2　If I bought £30 worth of rope, how long would it be?

A1 Do CM 64.

A2 Use the graph to find out how many zogs you would get for

a £70　　**b** £45　　**c** £82

A3 Use the graph to find out how many pounds you would get for

a 450 zogs　　**b** 890 zogs

Many countries measure their road distances in kilometres rather than miles.

This graph can be used to convert between both types of measurements.

Use it to answer the questions that follow.

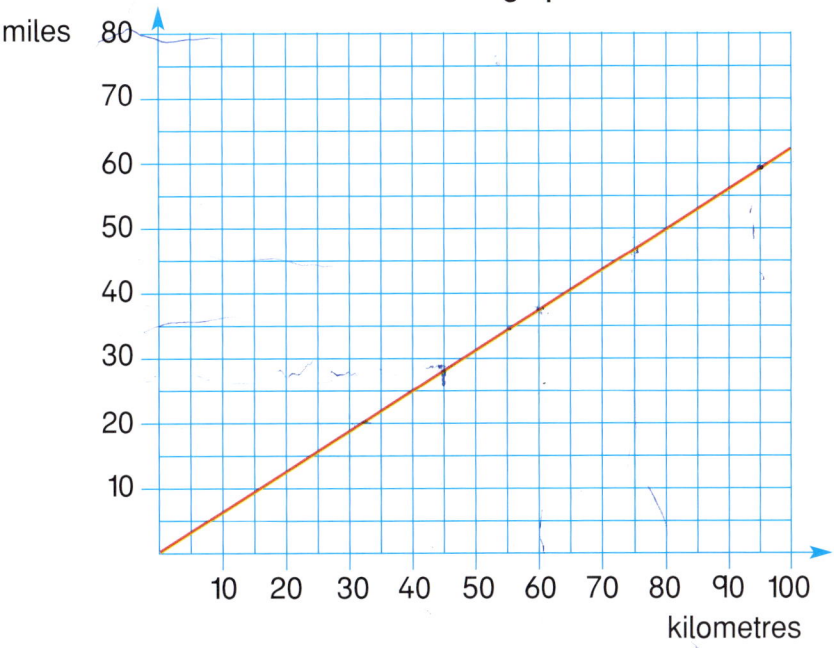

Conversion graph

(graph showing miles on vertical axis 0–80, kilometres on horizontal axis 0–100, with a straight line from origin through approximately (100, 60))

B1 How many miles would these distances be?

> Paris   60 km
> Rheims   45 km
> Troves   75 km

B2 How many kilometres would these be?

> Harlow   20 miles
> Chelmsford 55 miles
> Southend on Sea 80 miles

B3 Convert these distances to miles.

- a 40 km
- b 20 km
- c 70 km
- d 60 km
- e 55 km
- f 95 km

B4 Convert these distances to kilometres.

- a 10 miles
- b 20 miles
- c 28 miles
- d 62 miles

HD3 Organising and interpreting data 2

C1 Use the conversion graph to match up the road signs that show the same speeds.

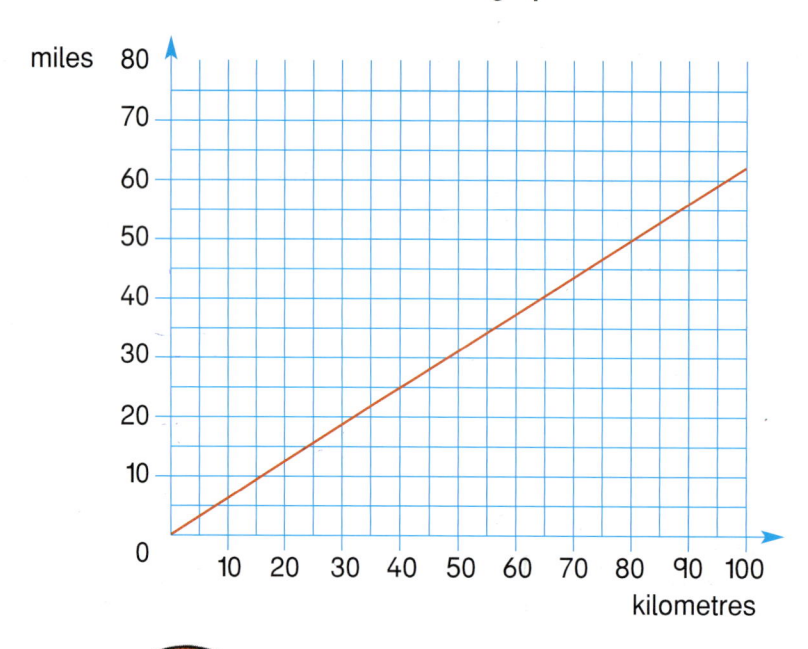

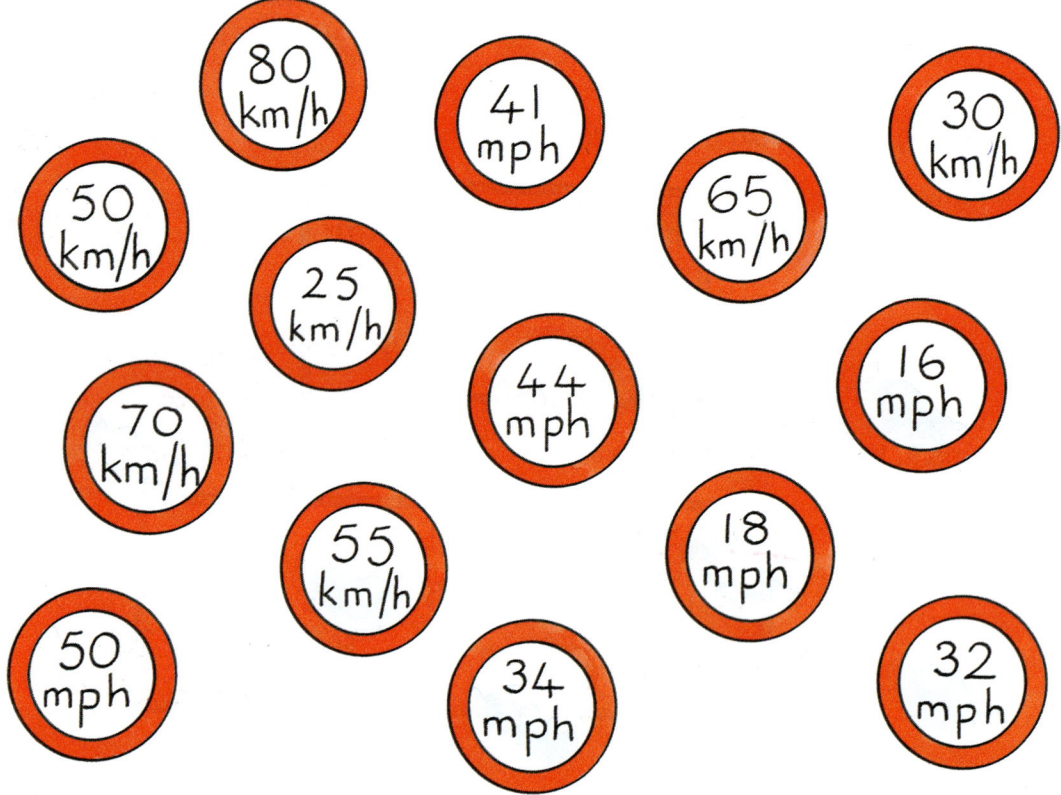

Conversion graph

Road signs:
- 80 km/h
- 41 mph
- 30 km/h
- 50 km/h
- 65 km/h
- 25 km/h
- 16 mph
- 70 km/h
- 44 mph
- 55 km/h
- 18 mph
- 50 mph
- 34 mph
- 32 mph

You need road atlases.

C2 Find some distances between towns that you know.

Convert them from miles to kilometres.

Key idea	Line graphs can be used to find intermediate values.

HD3 Organising and interpreting data 2

HD4.2 Mean, median, mode and range 3

> **Key idea**: The mean can be used to make comparisons between 2 sets of data.

The Clark family are deciding whether to go to America or Spain for their holiday this year. One of the things they will consider is the mean cost of certain items. Below are the equivalent costs in pounds and pence.

America

Sun Valley
Cola 80p
1 litre of petrol 20p

Palm Beach
Cola £1
1 litre of petrol 35p

Discovery Cove
Cola 95p
1 litre of petrol 32p

Paradise Island
Cola 85p
1 litre of petrol 28p

Spain

Bounty Bay
Cola 50p
1 litre of petrol 50p

Clearwater Beach
Cola 46p
1 litre of petrol 42p

Longboat Island
Cola 70p
1 litre of petrol 43p

Sunville
Cola 55p
1 litre of petrol 37p

★1 Work out the mean cost of cola in America by adding together all the cola prices from the American resorts. Repeat to find the mean cost of cola in Spain.

★2 Find the mean cost of a litre of petrol in America and in Spain.

A1 What is the range of costs for 1 litre of petrol in

   a America?   b Spain?

HD4 Organising and interpreting data 3

America

Sun Valley Beach lounger £1 Hamburger and chips £3.70 Child entrance to theme park £8.50
Palm Beach Beach lounger £1.20 Hamburger and chips £4.20 Child entrance to theme park £9.75
Discovery cove Beach lounger £1.15 Hamburger and chips £3.85 Child entrance to theme park £8.95
Paradise Island Beach lounger £1.28 Hamburger and chips £4.15 Child entrance to theme park £9.40

Spain

Bounty Bay Beach lounger £1.80 Hamburger and chips £5.20 Child entrance to theme park £6.28
Clearwater Beach Beach lounger £1.75 Hamburger and chips £4.80 Child entrance to theme park £6.33
Longboat Island Beach lounger £1.83 Hamburger and chips £5.95 Child entrance to theme park £7.30
Sunville Beach lounger £1.53 Hamburger and chips £3.68 Child entrance to theme park £5.55

A2 Copy and complete this table by calculating the mean costs of the items.

	Mean cost in America	Mean cost in Spain
Beach lounger		
Hamburger and chips		
Child entrance to theme park		

A3 What is the median cost of hamburger and chips in America and Spain?

B1 Use a collection of travel brochures.

Choose 1 holiday resort and select 5 different hotels from that resort. Design and set up a simple database to compare hotel prices in different months.

a Calculate the mean price of a hotel for 7 nights in April.

b Repeat **a** for August and September.

C1 Choose a different resort, perhaps in a different country, and repeat B1.

C2 Compare the prices of your 2 resorts. Which has the lowest mean price for each month?

What is the range of prices in each resort in a given month?

ID4.3 Interpreting and comparing data

> **Key idea** Different forms of data presentation can give different information.

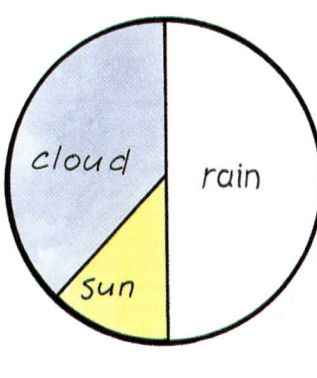

Weather on Monday — cloud, rain, sun

Weather on Tuesday — sun, cloud, snow

Weather on Wednesday — sun, snow, cloud

★
- **a** Which day had most cloud?
- **b** What fraction of Monday had rain?
- **c** What does the pie chart tell you about the weather on Tuesday?

1
- **a** When did it snow for $\frac{1}{3}$ of a day?
- **b** Which 2 days had the same amount of sunshine?
- **c** Which of these days would you choose for a long walk? Why?

2 This pie chart shows what Andy did on Wednesday.

Andy's day — sleeping, watching t.v., playing, homework, school, eating

- **a** What took most of his time?
- **b** What fraction of the day was spent at school?
- **c** Did he spend longer eating or watching TV?

3 How many hours did he spend at school?
What percentage of the day was this?

4 If watching TV takes $\frac{1}{8}$ of the chart, how many hours does this represent?

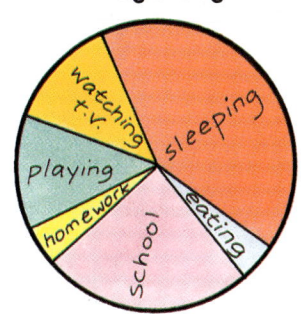

Remember, there are 24 hours in a day.

HD4 Organising and interpreting data 3

5 These charts show the amount of sunshine for two different weeks at the same holiday hotel.

Weather in week A

Weather in week B

If you could choose, which week would you think would be best for a holiday?

Week B

6 These bar charts show information about the same two weeks:

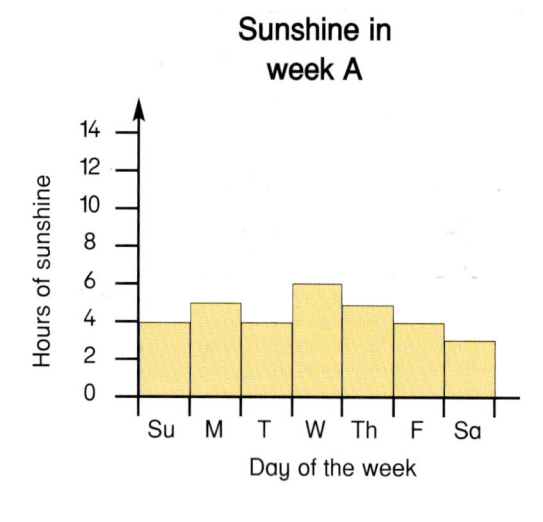

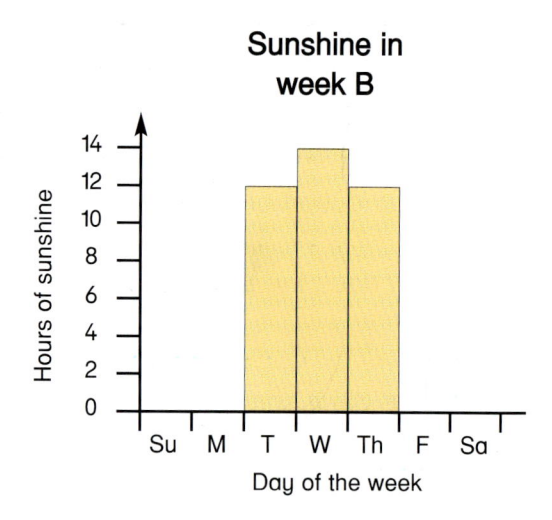

Sunshine in week A

Sunshine in week B

Would you still choose the same week to go on holiday? Explain your reasons.

yes it has got a bigger on 3 days

C1 Write down all the information about weeks A and B from the charts in questions 5 and 6, writing which chart gave you the information.

| Key idea | Different forms of data presentation can give different information. |

102 HD4 Organising and interpreting data 3

ID4.4 Line graphs 3

Key idea | Line graphs can be used to find unknown values.

★1 1 kg is about the same as 2.2 lb. Use this conversion chart to help you copy and complete the following table.

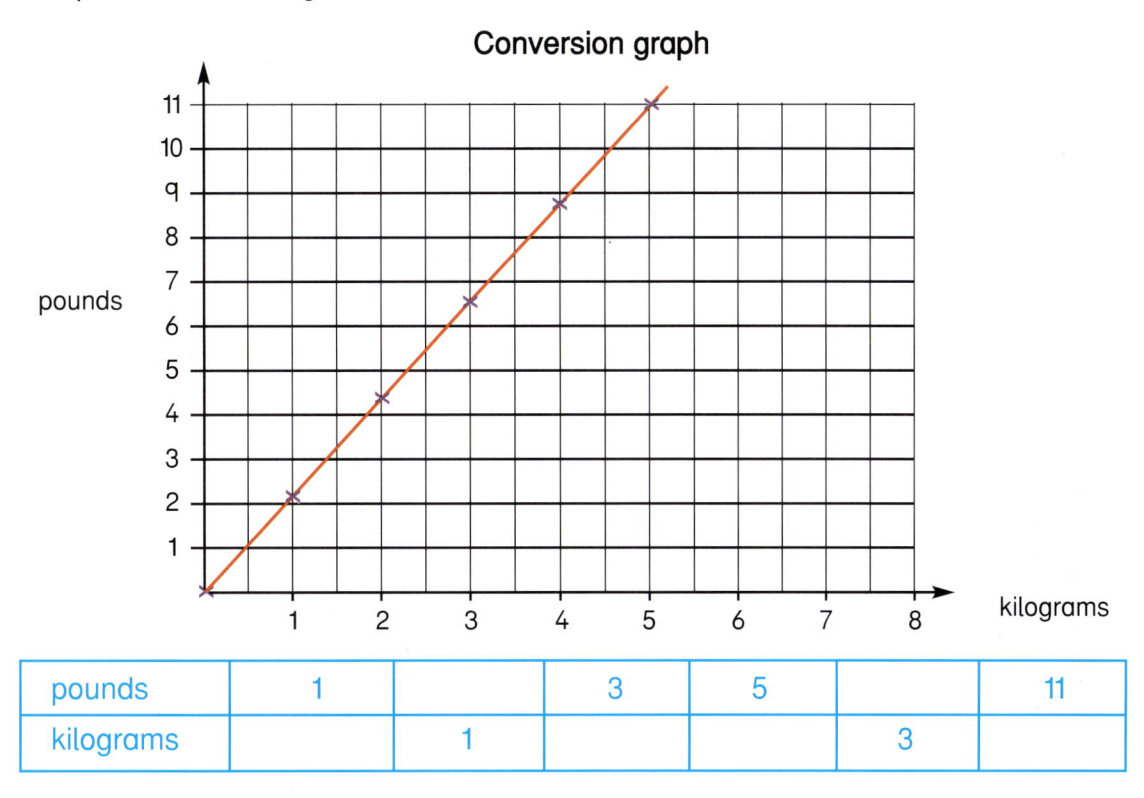

Conversion graph

pounds	1		3	5		11
kilograms		1			3	

B1 In Trinidad they use the dollar as their unit of currency. You get about 9 Trinidad dollars for £1.

Use this conversion graph to help you answer the questions.

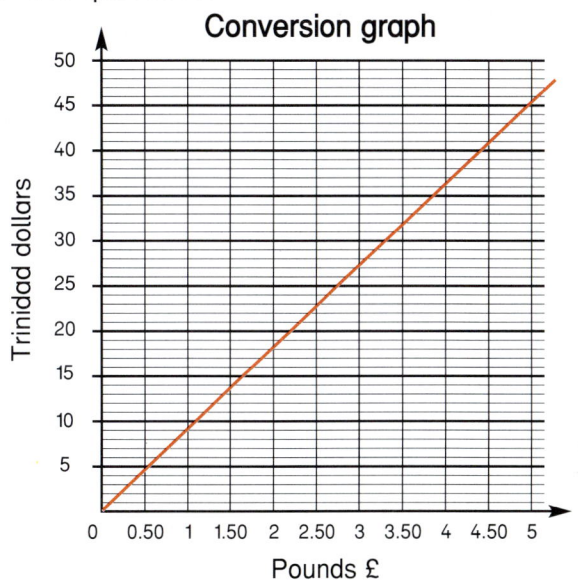

Roughly how many Trinidad dollars is

a £3?   **b** £4?   **c** £1.50?

Roughly how many pounds is

d 45 dollars?

e 18 dollars?

f 32 dollars?

HD4 Organising and interpreting data 3

B2 You need graph paper.

Temperatures can be measured in degrees Celsius and degrees Fahrenheit.

Draw a set of axes and plot these points.
0°C = 32°F   10°C = 50°F   35°C = 95°F

Join them up to make a line.

B3 Use your graph to help you copy and complete these tables which show monthly average temperatures.

Month	Jan	Feb	Mar	Apr	May	Jun	Jul	Aug	Sep	Oct	Nov	Dec
Mean temp (°C)		5	11			22	26		25		18	
Mean temp (°F)	35			60	67			85		64		43

C1 You need graph paper.

Small lengths can be measured in inches or centimetres.

One inch is roughly 2.5 centimetres.

Draw a graph to convert inches to centimetres.

C2 You need objects to measure.

Measure the lengths of some objects in centimetres. Use your graph to convert these measurements into inches.

C3 You need a ruler with inches on.

Measure the objects again in inches. How close were your conversions?

Key idea Line graphs can be used to find unknown values.